Treasure Hidden

A JOURNEY OF FAITH IN CHRIST

Pedrameh Manoochehri

WESTBOW
PRESS®
A DIVISION OF THOMAS NELSON
& ZONDERVAN

WestBow Press books may be ordered through booksellers or by contacting:

WestBow Press
A Division of Thomas Nelson & Zondervan
1663 Liberty Drive
Bloomington, IN 47403
www.westbowpress.com
1 (866) 928-1240

All Scripture quotations, unless otherwise indicated, are taken from New Revised Standard Version Bible, copyright © 1989 National Council of the Churches of Christ in the United States of America. Used by permission. All rights reserved worldwide.

Scripture quotations marked (KJV) taken from the King James Version of the Bible.

ISBN: 978-1-9736-6246-4 (sc)
ISBN: 978-1-9736-6245-7 (e)

Print information available on the last page.

WestBow Press rev. date: 06/20/2019

Contents

Highest Glory

Prologue

Hello reader and welcome to my journey. This book first began in a time of trial two years ago. It documents my journey of faith in Christ for the last eight years of my life. In the spring of 2011, this New Age-y high school art teacher was living a double life of sin and "righteousness," completely oblivious of a Father God reigning in heaven, much less the Trinity. She came to receive Christ and the Holy Spirit in faith. For someone experienced in the use of mind-altering drugs, I had no explanation for the extremely powerful and precise supernatural experiences that transformed my life. I learned to live for sobriety and for a God whose love I never realized or knew until Jesus revealed His being and heart to me.

His love changed me more radically than I ever could have imagined. I never would have given thought to some concept so grand as a divine destiny. But, He introduced me to such a purpose, declaring I was to help unite man under His cross. It took me so long to develop understanding of salvation. Now I am amazed at the tremendous reality framing our lives. From the start of mankind, God's wisdom purposed salvation by His own blood as a frame of redemption for man from sin and evil. The story of His chosen people, Israel, was extended to mankind by the cross of His Son, Jesus Christ. In His open arms, Jew and Gentile are received in the Father's Love.

I was one, amongst so many, to know this grace and come into this extraordinary knowledge. For this privilege, I hope this testament of my conversion and faith journey can draw you into what I've learned for the sake of salvation and honoring the grace of God with our lives. As you will discover, I have not lived this honor out in my own life and have suffered the consequence of my failure. The insecurity of my soul and sanctity has challenged my life immensely. The latter half of my story details this trial and the effort to redeem that destiny spoken over me so many years ago.

My journey has not been like so many I've seen and heard: one of grace received and born out righteously. Some of this was a result of my naïveté, ignorance, and simple, fallible humanity. Some of it was a result of irresponsibility and recklessness with the precious gift of the Cross. I hope sharing my lessons learned will both inspire courage and faith in you as well as warn and deter you from falling into similar errors and sins. While story comes to an "end" in this book, I am very much still in the midst of this journey, just barely beginning the hope of a purpose in God. It is no guarantee, but I hope to do my words and warnings justice. Ultimately, I hope for myself as I hope for you to surrender to a life written by the will and grace of God, to live for our Treasure, the Lord Jesus Christ.

There is no fear in love, but perfect love casts out fear;
for fear has to do with punishment, and whoever fears
has not reached perfection in love. 1 John 4:18

" GOD DOESN'T SEND fear" (But, I am sad. And scared.) People have spoken this truth as an assurance over me so many times. God is love. He doesn't send fear. Only the devil sends fear. I had trouble accepting this too simply in my personal experience. Searching the scriptures revealed to me a God of grace *and* judgment.

I couldn't put it together. But John said, perfect love casts out fear, for fear has to do with punishment, and God was our Savior. Even He said, He came not to Judge, but to Save. *I have come as light into the world, so that everyone who believes in me should not remain in the darkness. I do not judge anyone who hears my words and does not keep them, for I came not to judge the world, but to save the world. John 12:46-47*

So, why am I scared? Because I just am. Deep down. I cling to my blanket, hot tea, people, a jacket, precious things. Each a comfort to tide me over to the next. Time lasting forever it seems. Yet, so hasty. So rushed and restless. I listen to praise music, despite the fall in faith.

The song I'm listening to tonight is called "Pieces." It's about the heart of the Lord Jesus. I love that name. Beautiful name. Yet, it's been so wounded in me. I ended up growing bitter deep down. This woman, this daughter of God, sings: *Love is sacred, Love is pure, Love keeps it's word.* I can't argue with it. He is Love, beyond which was no other. There is no greater or deeper expression of Pure Love. A person.

It's hard to wrap one's mind around it. And mine fails constantly. Prior to this trial, joy in my Lord fed a heart of gratitude that spent the days meditating on His pure goodness and generosity. It was so powerful and overwhelming that the word "zeal" was surely created for the purpose of describing the heart's inclination towards God in the love He inspires. They say, the joy of the Lord is one's strength. True, true.

In that season of old, I used to be so zealous that I'd collect His praises piece by piece through each day, tallying them by night in a "praise report" to thank Him for this thing and that one. My mind would always be amazed—another day, and I can't believe how many gifts I've collected thank you's for. And I'd think, well, that's Him. It's to be expected, of course. Yet, for the finite, limited little me, I was for my part amazed. I can only imagine how small it seems to Him. So vast.

Like my computer screen sporting a photo of a sunlit mountain range capped with snow. Vast. A friend of mine once said she was marveling at such a scene on a camping trip and asked God, "Why?" He answered, "Because I just felt like it. I like it." Of course! When you're God, well, "just because" is all the answer we need. In the second book of Torah, Exodus (3:14), He instructed Moses: *Thus you shall say to the Israelites, 'I AM has sent me to you.'* No, you don't need a name. He just Is.

Unworthy! I Am Unworthy. Well, of course you are. It's inevitably constructed that way. Everyone's unworthy. Yet, Mercy brings a blessed family home to heaven. As for me, I can barely look at His name I typed. And I was supposed to write a book about His grace on my life! Courage from where? Guts from where? From the same place my stubborn will resides. My father's side of our family is Jewish. The scriptures certainly testify to a people with a rebellious streak. I take some solace in this much, even if they never fared well for it. So, I suppose I'll just lay the blame for my temperament on my heritage as stubborn people are wont to do and take a stab at this book of grace anyway.

So, here's the story of my faith journey...

BORN AGAIN

The Word in the Wilderness

I KEPT TRYING TO go to Starbuck's like I used to in the first few years of my faith walk. It was my scripture study "office." Many mornings, in this season of old, I'd wait at the door as they first opened, excited at another day I get to read! A blessing born again each pitch dark morning. This practice marked my days with joy. The passion I had for spending time with God in this way anchored and strengthened me. Eventually, however, the Lord was ready to move on, and I wasn't. I pursued this study ritual so stubbornly, against His will, that I've hardly studied for the last year at all. This alone was a grief and a death in me.

My faith and passion for reading the Bible came to take up so much space in my heart that I didn't realize it's scope until the layers were stripped one by one. Who knew how much this zealous faith of mine had displaced from my heart? I was certainly oblivious. I never really imagined heart "real estate" like I've discovered in this trial. All this territory was ceded to the study of scripture in a hungry search for understanding and a new sense of devotion to my heritage. Never mind I could spend time with my Lord at my own will. The more time I spent with Him, the more I wanted.

Noble or innocent as this may seem, I sinned to cling to my Bible. Surely, God didn't call anyone, much less His own, to make studying more of a priority than the very people such study would aim to serve. When asked, *Teacher, how does one inherit eternal life?* He answered, *Love the Lord your God with all your heart, mind, and strength; and, love your neighbor as yourself.*

Love. Love God, one another, and yourself. According to Proverbs, the human spirit is the lamp of the Lord, searching the inward being. I always imagine He's the witness to all things, most especially my dishonor towards a person. So, the point is to love God and people most of all, not love your Bible more than your family. I was clutching my fix, a Word-addict.

I refused to release it since moving to The Woodlands. Just like the Israelites in Exodus, I've been through a wilderness season here. I should know better than to trust a town with such a name! Mind you it's beautiful and cut through with bike trails so we're hardly surviving a brutal pilgrimage eating manna or anything. Just suffering an order to exit Starbucks. Nevertheless, I'd be sitting at my little table, book open and insistent, when I'd suddenly see this robed figure I *love* a little too much, my Love is walking out the door—saying in essence, I'm leaving you, I don't agree with this.

He said, *Those who follow Me will walk in the light of life.* Boy did I learn that the hard way. Follow Him out of the Starbucks! Nope. I protested: *But, I'm studying Your very Word!* The prophets, no less, were my concern at the time. When you lament in sympathy with the heart and grief of the book of Lamentations, it sure feels justified. Never mind the comparison is an offense to the circumstance these souls faced. The suffering that ever birthed the laments of the Old Testament are well beyond any life I've ever known but on a newspaper cover or a computer screen. Nevertheless, on went my anxieties: *But, if I leave this place, I don't know what else to do.* Literally.

I had just moved to my parents hometown, and so, I had no structure to the day. My father was providing an apartment by grace until I could afford to get on my feet. I had no idea what to do with myself after being let go from a job at a nearby hardware store the week before. My first day on the job, I started to cry in the middle of checking out a customer. It was the second such cry within the hour. A coworker asked if I needed a break outside. Collecting myself facing the parking lot, I confessed to a consoling supervisor—I hear voices that speak cruel things over me.

Years of this same head space. This "trial" started within the first year of converting. No amount of rebuking evil spirits, prayer, or deliverance studies have released me completely. Much of the torment and attacks have ceased over these years little by little, but that day, I still cracked under the pressure of learning a register. The manager watched as I tried to search digital menus through a barrage of misogynistic insults and cut downs berating my brain. How do you explain such a thing to anyone but another familiar with it, much less in the official context of a new job?

Somehow, I actually managed to teach high school for a year and half in the same head space. Though the torment was far worse then, I was in a job that had blessed me with supportive staff and students that knew me well enough to love and overlook their teacher's quirks. At that time, earlier on in the battle, I'd sense the presence of these spiritual entities throwing literal verbal barbs at my body as if there were a cloud of them about me. The Bible describes how the "fiery darts" of the enemy are to be quenched upon the shield of faith. That "faith" is literally His actual presence, a shield of light I've experienced that does quite literally "quench" the barbs.

This one time, the Lord saved me by a special prayer. I had just arrived to fulfill my volunteer shift at this Christian coffeeshop. I told the manager I had to leave, that it was too difficult. He insisted on gathering the brothers. Everyone circled me to pray. Afterwards, one young man came around to my table in the back and said, "God's asked me to talk with you."

He proceeded to share his personal testimony of involvement in darkness, and even Satanism for a time, before surrendering his life to Christ. He described torments I thought were surely unique to my freak existence. Such strange sorceries and vile darkness that I felt isolated and singular. I was shocked and grateful for his words. He then asked to pray for me. I accepted gladly. So he took my hand in his and lifted a simple, sweet prayer up to God.

Then, he went on his way, and I regained enough hope to take up my barista duties with a heartened manager encouraging me on. The rest of that whole shift I felt enveloped in an egg shaped bubble of light I could see glowing fuzzy bright about me. I could hear the barbs faintly and feel their aim, but they were literally extinguished when they hit that shield. Ephesians 6:16 says, *With all of these, take the shield of faith, with which you will be able to quench all the flaming arrows of the evil one.* And Psalm 27:5 states, *For he will hide me in his shelter in the day of trouble; he will conceal me under the cover of his tent; he will set me on a high rock.*

The Rock of Ages, Christ. I felt so empowered and happy. Utterly relieved and grateful. Oh, that each day would be like this! These darts were physically wounding rather than just psychologically hurtful. They were painful and exhausting to bear up. Especially while trying to teach a class and serve students individually.

I used to teach high school art. I got used to concentrating and focusing my attention on the person and task at hand with a determined constancy. It never seemed to let up. I do recall finding comfort in the company of friends or familiar places I enjoyed. There were respites, and certainly love and zeal, to offset the torment. But it was intense. The darts ceased a couple years ago, but the mental berating grew worse at times. I clung the harder to my habits and any stable and comforting items I could hold onto.

Since then, it has become hard to read scripture like I once held to as a rock. So, over the last year or two, I started listening to preachers and watching programs. My normally able and clear mind became muddled with a strange sort of dyslexia and a twisting of my thoughts. Never would I imagine a curse occurring so clearly. This simply cannot be biology, unfortunately. Needless to say, I couldn't quite read the same.

So, audio and visual learning replaced the written word more and more. In this new alternate realm of study, I heard countless testimonies of people's lives and how their path brought them to know the Lord and His work in their person. I learned there's a whole world of knowledge tied to the spirit realm, perhaps not as detailed in some ways as the wisdom and history of the scriptures, but certainly rich with the lived reality of people in the present day.

Amazingly, these lives correspond to the scriptures just like my experience of the "shield of faith" was a testimony of God's reality and power in prayer. In their personal generosity, so many have shared experiences that are hard to put words to or tie back to a doctrine or philosophy; yet, story after story reflects a reality of life saved by the same God, but by means sometimes beyond the reach of reason.

For example, while scientists correlate genetic influence with a tendency to alcoholism, there is an understanding in the realm of faith that describes a reality of generational curses that find their cure in deliverance rather than chemistry. Troubles like alcoholism, divorce, abuse, drugs or theft are passed down by the "sins of the father," so to speak, an account never cleared that ends up troubling a bloodline. Devoted servants of the Lord seek to free such souls by honoring the Lord's sacrifice for their sake in deliverance ministry.

Of the many wondrous works of the Lord, this freedom was the first declaration of His identity in the gospels. The book of Luke describes this scene. One day during service in the synagogue, He arose and read a piece of prophecy from Isaiah declaring his true identity to the congregation. After having lived among his community as a son of the carpenter Joseph, the Messiah proclaimed, "I have come to set the captives free."

In the book of me: And the people, sitting in the hushed silence of the moment, considered, *Who? The carpenter's son, literally?* Yes. As it was said, "A prophet finds no honor in his home town." *Wasn't he the son of and the brother of and that young man known for his diligence and goodness in the neighborhood? We've watched him grow up since... What speaks this man?*

Well, a tremendous word of prophecy and some good news, ultimately, for souls suffering in the prison of sickness, injustice, and generations of cursing, especially. I'm one yet to overcome fully, and I'm just barely starting to grasp the magnitude of "the gospel." Truly, so many captives, and One sufficient for all.

It's the most amazing knowledge to try to comprehend. Even His own supernova's—from the reaches of the cosmos to the infinite world of the microscopic life in the ocean, with its strange and wonderful creatures too deep but for modern means of discovery—all speak to a creation served in a knowledge even greater than that which could be collected from it's study.

Psalm 19:1-4 states, *The heavens are telling the glory of God; and the firmament proclaims his handiwork. Day to day pours forth speech, and night to night declares knowledge. There is no speech, nor are there words; their voice is not heard; yet their voice goes out through all the earth, and their words to the end of the world.*

His was a story of grace. Grace came by a Name to pay the price of any penalty, but that you trust and receive that God takes justice that seriously and lays the reality of mercy bare for all the world to try to fathom Him.

His Way Is Perfect

PSALM 18:30 WAS one of my favorites when I was zealously immersed as a David in love with the Word. I longed to master the wisdom of God that I should please Him. And of course, I loved praise. Celebrating my Lord for His goodness was about the most uplifting thing I ever knew. Psalms of praise were especially pleasing to me. This one states, *This God—his way is perfect.* Perfection that perhaps considers "I want to see beautiful mountains cutting deep valleys into the world; and so, it shall be."

I try to get up in the morning and make of myself a pleasing enough sight, matching this and that appropriately, digging out proper earrings. When I accomplish this, I am pleased, in me. I did good! Among other banal moments of daily victory as a puny human. He's so daunting. Technically, I ought to curl up in the crook of His being so vast is He to my teeny.

If, for example, that feral kitten I held one morning, trying to console it's tiny being—if she had feared me for my size, how disappointed I would have been. How I'd longed for her to receive me, filled with sympathy and unable to be other than I am. Right after moving into this apartment, my friend phoned me about a kitten she rescued. Do you want it? Yes! I knew that cat was my savior technically. A gift from God to anchor my hurt heart down to love.

My friend and her family came by and helped this little girl settle in. We set up her litter box and milk and water bowls. It was clear she needed to see a vet first thing in the morning. That night, I tried over hours to court her permission for me to even touch her. One eye was swollen shut with infection. She was so hurt, curled into herself in the corner of her cage covered with fleas. I extended my hand into it's door and waited for any sign. A sniff of my fingers maybe? Nope. She was immovable, unconsolable.

I tried to sleep, assuring myself: get rest for the morning trip to the vet. Then, this nagging feeling. I'm not doing as I ought to be doing. What is it Lord? *Hold her.* Really? But she's not receiving me. *Just reach in, pick her up, and wrap her in that towel.* Ok, if You say so. I was leaned against a wall of my patio, next to her cage. I reached in and picked her up gently, tentatively—hesitant of her reaction. I thought, *just do it!*

I swaddled her in this towel on my chest and just held her. I couldn't believe what happened. She *wanted* to be held, and I would never have realized she needed what she couldn't convey to me. She looked up into my eyes, longingly, searching out my soul it seemed. I felt barely worthy to even be holding this beautiful, fragile little suffering one; but, I searched her eyes out, too, in sympathy.

She was grateful. I felt absolutely unworthy of her love. I never would have known to do this, to just reach in and hold her. But for God. After a while, most shockingly, as I loosened the hug to see if she might be interested now in the milk she hadn't touched all night, I was taken aback by her sudden life! She got up from the folds of the towel and began walking bold circles around my neck.

She wasn't interested in nourishment. She had apparently taken heart—she was interested in stretching out her new life force. She walked wide circles around the patio, eyed the water bowls, and then, after a good stretch of confidence—she took some sips, checked out her litter box, looked around like she was owning it! Well then. I would never have known how much love could affect this teeny being. Love leading to hope leading to faith, and in faith, all the boldness of our victory—this our victory in God! See, His way is perfect.

For the love of God is this, that we obey his commandments. And his commandments are not burdensome, for whatever is born of God conquers the world. And this is the victory that conquers the world, our faith. Who is it that conquers the world but the one who believes that Jesus is the Son of God? 1 John 5:3-5

For the one who proclaims Christ? What about the unbeliever who sees a creation men are but stewarding in the responsibility of reason? I was as much before converting. An unwitting, unintentional atheist who believed in "the Universe" and the supernatural power of Truth. So, I wonder such things. How many atheists abide in a humility before creation putting the self righteous and proud believer to shame? I have been this believer at turns in my life since converting seven years ago. I've stumbled in my naïveté and amazement at this wisdom and instruction I'd missed out on all my life—but for the awakening by mercy and grace in middle age! Teaching high school at that.

Suddenly, I caught on to all those really good kids who looked disappointed in me at times. It was always a mystery to me. What am I doing wrong? I felt bad. I really wanted to serve my kids rightly, and I knew they were too kind to make mention of my wrongs. Then, I awoke to a curriculum that wasn't exactly holy. My discipline was also short of righteous correction. After converting, it was suddenly clear—*Oooh, those are the Christian kids! They fear the Lord. No wonder they're so good.* And I was so caring in many ways. No wonder they were confused by me.

Now, I realize I wasn't all bad prior to converting and neither were the other kids "bad" kids. Also, it's probably not fair to hold every Christian child to the "good" mold. But, most of them were really good kids. So, this was a reality nevertheless, which is itself a testament to growing up in the instruction of the Lord. For what it's worth, never did I feel so loved and respected by anyone as I did by my Jesus after I first converted.

One day, I was so pressed by the demands of the classroom that I escaped to the bathroom down the hall to collect myself. In the quiet of my being, I heard Him say, *I know your struggle.* He consistently showed me that he appreciated my genuine love and effort to reach each child as deeply as I was able to muster, that He loved me. Gentile, heathen, unbelieving atheist agnostic as I may have been but a matter of months earlier. Beyond time and judgment, I consider His love for each child in that room, no matter how they're being raised.

As I was, I never quite succeeded in imposing a fearsome authority to win the respect of my kids. There was always a measure of: Look, I'm loveably entertaining in my humors and charms, no? Just do it for Ms. M, please. Always this wheeling and dealing element in my efforts to compensate for any lack of stature in my person—size, age, knowledge, wisdom, gender, etc. as the case may have been—depending on what it seemed to take in my perception. *Oh,* said my reason, maturing to catch on to the root of my troubles—*that sub was a tall man in his sixties who once served in the military. Of course.* Teens in humble submission. So easy the flow of a day when they respect the teacher's authority. *Go figure. Don't take it personal. You can't manage that anyway, and still be yourself.*

I know because I tried and tried to be other people, and it always failed. *Just admire and assimilate traits best you can and move on, being you.* So I did my best with my personal toolbox of tricks and traits. I managed to float as many peaceful, productive days as I could down the river of a school year. Boy can that stretch of time try everyone getting along on the ark. Animals I tell you. Noah, the righteous teach in the lead, included.

But hey, learn some basics in art making we did! Some days I even took immense pride to look upon an absolute exception to the rule of chaos and winging it so many days felt like—rows of students so engaged in creating mandala paintings that the silent scene stunned me. They were on such a roll that I actually excused myself from the room and just left the thirty or so teens to skip across the hallway to my coworkers' room. I confessed my excitement to somebody who'd appreciate the miracle. For real, it's like this, Julie! She shared in my moment.

Julie was special, the mother of so many in this small city-in-a-building. For one day a year her room sported a red cross on the door as it became the "mum hospital." Mums are a Texas football tradition for the homecoming game. On this day, mum-adorned students swam down the hallway between classes in a stream of ribbons rustling and bells jingling. Julie's room bore the beacon of hope and help for girls sporting especially lavish mums, ill supported by a mere blouse.

This woman was so rightfully beloved that she hosted students of all walks, art or otherwise, in her room before school began. Showing up an hour early for the day, the room teemed with kids chatting quietly while working on homework. Pure love. Talk about a mentor to grow under in your first teaching job. She fielded my every need on call for the whole five years I was there.

Most of the time, I'd be running across the hallway of students, cutting my jagged edge over to ask a quick piece of advice on some matter or other. She'd been teaching for 24 years when I started. She was a stunning artist who got her Art I students to create amazing work that shocked the eyes. So, when she didn't field my need for counsel, she was often the first to know my joy at some moment of success or pride in my kids.

This day of the mandalas really stands out because it was, essentially, a miracle. For the short term of my career I'd never seen such a classroom sight. Like that moment I imagine moms may feel when the clutter and chaos of an average day's play suddenly falls eerily silent. I looked up from whatever I was doing at my teacher desk with a multitasking awareness watching for trouble or a hand raised and found instead rows of silence and work.

Hmmm. What is this? Quiet decisions and efforts? There they were, all too busy to even notice we were missing our accomplishing-as-goofing-off mark I seemed to foster in my "classroom management" style. Instead, they sat painting with painstaking diligence for craft's sake. Weighing color relationships and mixing decisions with the gravity of an artist. Offering serious and sincere feedback to a neighbor. A teacher's dream. An ideal I wouldn't have imagined witnessing for all the crazy our class ever was in the name of freedom, fun, and creativity.

Most days, there was a range of social dynamics too powerful for a work ethic to overwhelm the overall complexity of interactions. A wide variety of kids filled the seats—athletes, artists, scientists, political scientists, and so on. Unbeknownst to any onlooker, there they sat arranged in the awkward social engineering effort I drafted called the teacher "seating chart." This was only if they couldn't manage a peaceful order independently.

I'd try to strategically place them in particular ways to support concentration and positive feedback, sometimes successfully merging nerds with athletes to my delight. Other times, I found the expression Jesus used about a bit of yeast leavening the whole dough to be true. Rather than the serious, diligent students influencing the less behaved ones positively, I ended up spreading chaos evenly through the room. Can't tell what may come of it. And it's fun, too. To watch the quieter students loosen up under the influence of the more raucous ones was often a pleasant, unexpected outcome. This was typical of the whimsy I enjoyed weaving into my classroom.

After committing my life to Christ, however, I came to reflect on at least some of my curricular choices very differently. For example, the Day of the Dead cultural lesson on the Mexican holiday was just a bit out there. I wondered why some of the girls were opposed to painting skulls, for heavens sake. I was blind as they say. It was to honor ancestors in their passing, of course. But one girl's mom didn't see any of that—just that her daughter's assignment was to watercolor a giant skull.

These sorts of choices wove their way into my presentations and assignments in my ignorance towards the way of the Lord. Children raised up in the instruction of the Lord was a whole new, radical concept to me as I began getting deeper into the scriptures and reflecting on their wisdom. My curriculum, likewise, began to change in accord with this whole new frame of mind. His way was definitely not the one I ever knew, and I couldn't argue with it. His way was transforming me.

Born Again

THE BEGINNING OF this commitment introduced me to that reality I'd heard referenced by someone somewhere sometime. The scales had fallen off my eyes the very morning I commit myself standing there in my kitchen. The night before I had watched this testimony of a woman's encounter with the Lord. She had been warned of those who have come to know Him, but end up walking in a direction that is not with Him but moving away from Heaven towards Hell.

It dawned on me, what if that's me? I was shaking, mortified of the possibility in the conviction of my conscience. I had already come to the Lord in faith. I was writing Him letters and praying, but I had not even invested in a Bible or made any kind of commitment. I went to sleep wondering of my fate and my loved ones, journaling my concerns. I left off in my journal asking this very question, what about my loved ones? Knowing my own choice solidly, of course. I would follow the Lord.

I awoke to find this red paper heart laying over my journal entry. I knew intuitively it was meant to answer my question: *Just love them.* That's my job, to simply love them. The rest was beyond my concern. Salvation is scary. But I felt assured still. I wondered of the heart. Where had it been? Buried in papers? How did it get there? Angels. I was somewhat awed, though I believed in angels. Anyway, it was this morning, the first day of summer, that I broke down at some point standing against the kitchen counter, sensing His presence leaning against the fridge to the side of me. I started to cry at this sense of remembrance. I knew He knew me better than anyone could ever come to know me in my life.

I sensed my condition—strayed and lost of my origin, my childhood innocence, my true self and being. I'd adopted all this conditioning, this personality and persona. Layers I'd put on adapting to life's challenges and demands, socially especially, to fit in and find belonging and love and friendship. I knew I'd strayed. I didn't realize this before. It dawned on me as a new awareness that struck me deeply.

I realized, *I love Him so much.* I distinctly missed Him. How? He was a completely new aspect of my life then. I had come into faith that spring—in fact, it was exactly the first day of spring and this day was the first day of summer. That spring night, I simply believed He was God. I was journaling late and into the early morning, reflecting fervently on life. Suddenly this thought dawned on me, piercing my considerations: *I am not going to truly live and become the person I would want to be and respect without knowing God.*

By the end of this reflection, I decided to ask Him a question. I sensed, I am addressing Him as if He is God and is real and alive in my mind. I set out to try to word my question and got stuck trying to express it half way through. Then, my thought was completed by a "voice" actually originating in my heart. On top of that novel experience, the conclusion of the question was also the answer to the question. Woah. I was a bit taken aback. Ok, I guess He is real!

As I fell asleep I could feel a presence. The next morning driving to work, I felt a remarkable peace. I no longer had to control my foot of lead from pressing too hard on the gas, tapping the brakes and then the gas and so on. It stayed at a steady pace. All day I felt this strange peace cover me. We discovered some troubling news that morning—new teachers who had worked under three years may have their contracts terminated as our new superintendent reworked the budget. That was me and my coworker. We commiserated over the shock of it.

I felt so remarkably peaceful. I felt no anxiety about my lot, and sensed, I will be ok. Later on in my faith walk, I realized this was of God. The Lord's "peace blanket" as I came to call it. It's a tremendous grace and blessing. I haven't always enjoyed this since then. I think it was His way of affirming my faith in Him the night before, a confirmation of His reality as God. I was amazed. It was a rather overwhelming discovery then. From this point I began addressing Him more and more as I journaled, praying to Him for guidance in my person. I asked for help mostly, to become a better person, especially in my relationships.

It was this new relationship with the Lord I realized that summer night that I had neglected to honor with a commitment. I felt guilt and conviction suddenly. I had yet to put away alcohol, though I had sensed it was time to put it away. As I stood there in the kitchen that summer day, I was overcome with this absolute sadness that I should ever stray from Him again. It was a remembrance somehow. I knew in some sense that He was my origin. I had once belonged to Him, had come from Him and got lost of this reality somehow along the way of my life, 33 years by this point.

I knew He was my only hope of return and safety going forward. I never wanted to lose Him again. I couldn't afford it. I missed Him so much. I knew that I loved Him somehow deeper than I had realized. All this despite the new sense of relationship I had been walking in and experiencing. I understood I need to make a true and deep commitment to Him. I sensed Him with me, comforting and assuring me.

I left the house to buy a Bible from my favorite used bookstore. I would need to start learning about who He is from this day forward. For some reason, He chose this year of my life to make known to me His reality and being and my need. I often came to wonder why now, why in this manner? Why not my sister or parents? I had not one Christian friend, not that I knew of anyway. But, this much I've come to accept: no matter my questions or ignorance or wonder, His way is always perfect. In this I rest assured.

Far from Fear, Free

PROVERBS 9:10 STATES, *The fear of the Lord is the beginning of wisdom, and knowledge of the Holy One is understanding.* Well this concept, "the fear of the Lord" was rather confusing to me initially, even if I had plenty of it just to realize and imagine He is God. God knows everything all the time. Nothing is hidden from Him. And then, as if that isn't enough, He also happens to be perfect. Flawless in every regard, most especially in justice and wisdom.

I, on the other hand, hardly feel I am worth watching even if you are my Maker. I had spent all my adult life from about age seven onward in a sense of private existence. If I was alone, well, I was alone. No one else was around. There was no sense whatsoever in me that I am known and observed by any omniscient consciousness, much less His "hosts," the angels I now believe are assigned to souls for their well being. Nope, it was just me when no one was around.

That's how I'd ended up living such a compartmental existence by the time I came into faith. I called them hats. As a dual degree grad student, I'd put on my anthropology hat when I was with that department. I had another hat for art education, the other department I immersed my life in during that season. Eventually as a teacher, there was a hat for school, life at home, and time with friends. It never occurred to me to live a completely transparent life. I learned to keep my world partitioned in high school when I had some aspects of life that my parents just didn't need to know too well, or at all. I counted it as privacy adults are entitled to and never considered the concept it seemed God was opening up to me in coming to understand His reality just before converting.

The idea of freedom kept arising. Then one day, I opened the front door of my house before heading out to work and saw this random blank sheet of paper sitting on the front lawn, and what do know, the word "Freedom" was written big and bold across it. I had been journaling that morning about this very idea just before discovering it! I knew "life" was trying to speak to me. Soon enough, I realized there is a freedom in living transparently. Be the person you could be before anyone all day and feel at ease with who you choose to be at anytime. No compartments. Hats perhaps—can't be a teacher all day to everyone, but not the way I had been living. Happy hour me was a whole other person than the one leading class!

So, needless to say, 33-year-old me sported a measure of ignorance with regard to anything remotely scriptural, "Christian," religious, faith or anything in general to do with the world of such knowledge. I never made any effort to educate myself in such subjects, presuming of myself—I'm not a religious person, nor would I ever be. Much less Christian of all religions. For some reason, I implicitly presumed this religion was the one belonging to "those conservative people." I was actually closest to New Age if anything. I believed in life, the "Universe," and intuition as a sign of a spirit realm that does exist after all. I just didn't really populate it with any particular characters in my consideration. I did such things as "set my intention" and began increasingly to "declare my truth to the Universe."

I believed, of all things, that a thought or desire that was intimately and personally sincere and true had great power in existence. Some higher intelligence that organized reality received such truth and put its power into motion in my life. And it worked! I watched such declared desires come to pass. Now, of course, these are essentially prayers that God answered with respect, I suppose, for my good intent. Most such things were desires I had for my character and improvement as a person. Go figure! I suppose He would appreciate and answer such hopes. I just didn't imagine Truth was a particular Person. Good heavens! Uh, Jesus: *I am the Truth, the Way, and the Life*, He told his disciples and the crowds learning from his ministry. But even then, I'd never heard this expression. It was new to me!

As were certain realities such as: Jesus was a Jew. I literally wondered at one point what Christianity had to do with Jews. Now, I'm rather amazed at that moment I heard this one lady at Bunko night mention how she was beginning her Sabbath worship that Friday evening in preparation for synagogue the next day on Saturday to worship Jesus. Woah. This was news to me. I asked her—Wait a minute, what are you doing? What does Judaism have to do with church? Yup. She was a Messianic Jew who accepted Christ as the true Messiah and Son of God.

Anyway. I had trouble with many things I heard referenced with regularity on the Christian radio stations I started listening to all the time. I tuned in anytime I was driving or had the chance to hear more, more, more about Christianity. I stopped turning away those evangelists I used to close my front door on like they were vacuum salesman. I invited them in for tea instead. I wanted to learn what they had to share. I wanted to learn anything to do with this identity and commitment I had embraced.

Now that I'm a "Christian," for example, do I have to have every political stance align with my brethren if I even know what they might be? Do I have any clue what I believe about anything anymore? Do I have to have all my views personally hashed out to answer anyone to whom I might proclaim my new identity? Do I realize this "identity" amounts to nothing more complicated than being another sinner in need of a Savior? No.

Unfortunately, I didn't understand the simple, pure beauty of loving God. All you need to do or be is love. The only answer I owed anyone was my honest presence and confession of love if I chose to even share something so personal and valuable to me. I love Jesus for loving and saving me. The most simple version. But, did I know this early on in my faith walk? No. Instead, I hibernated for the first six months. I made no mention to anyone, save for my parents after about four months virtually alone.

Looking back, I savored this growing knowledge and intimacy over what became a honeymoon period essentially. While I felt the burden of owing answers I was ill prepared to understand, I did end up enjoying a private season. I wish I'd maintained that condition a bit more over the years, but indeed, my zeal eventually overwhelmed any sense of privacy I had once enjoyed. It was that feeling, much like falling in love, when you first begin to get more and more serious about a guy you really like but haven't quite confessed to your friends or loved ones. Just a special secret you're carrying about like a treasure inside. Then, slowly over time, you begin to confess this beautiful thing in awkward turns with more and more people.

My love affair began to crack open this one afternoon talking on the phone with my sister. From the time we were young, she was my first friend and, often, my best one. Apart from our catty battles in that season when I was about ten and she was six, we got along really well. Besides, those days we spent way too much time sharing the back seat of our family trips fueled by my father's ambitions as a road warrior and my parents' wanderlust.

Enough time in confined spaces and next thing you know, like animal kingdom, there's a territory battle ensuing over the middle seat between kin. *You crossed the line! Mooooom! Are you guys at it again? She pinched me!* I was usually the culprit in reality, but my parents tended to favor and glorify their first born in a ridiculous bias that my little sister bore rather gracefully over time. Now, of course, she's a beautifully humble and generous soul. All thanks to the cruelties endured.

On the brighter end of our history, I spent summer days preparing her the eternal lunch while she waited starving in the living room. I had to make the perfect plate for my precious sister to spoil her, you see. So I'd decorate it as a sculpture, and this took some time. *Is it done yet?! I'm hungry!* Almost, almost. And the next 10 minutes were spent arranging goldfish crackers in a holy circle around her sandwich and carrot sticks or what have you.

Any wonder the future art teacher would come to be related to a future attorney. My sister always had a knack for deciphering manuals, whether it was building furniture or solving the mysteries of electronic devices. Now she's a minister of the legal code. Much as the foreshadowing of our childhoods implied, we have our differences of temperament and life paths. On the other hand, we share the same handwriting, sound the same voice on an answering machine, and share a unique sense of humor that has earned me the rare and fortunate compliment. She insists that sometimes I'm the only one to laugh at her jokes, and she loves this about me. She's quite witty and humorous, so this is an accomplishment.

With all this said, she was my confidant. We talked nightly or even sometimes on our morning drives to work. This one night we were enjoying our evening chat as she drove home from work and I was chopping vegetables for dinner in the kitchen. The conversation was going along as usual, but our talks had been growing increasingly awkward as I was transforming and being consumed more and more in my relationship to the Lord.

I never brought Him up, never made any mention to my sister. I didn't want to disturb our dynamic. I cherished her. She and her husband identified as atheist. She said, we place our faith in science. They live beautiful godly lives in so many ways I've come to appreciate in Biblical terms over these years, so as far as I'm concerned they just haven't discovered they are actually better Christians than I've managed to be much of the time.

Years after zealously pouring over my precious Bible's crinkly pages, I've matured in reverse—discovering the arc of wisdom develops backward, back to being a child. As a child, I was always "home," in a way—alive and simple, in a world so deep and complex. My parents partied (pretty tame by my standards, nevertheless much fun was had) when I was young, but what a Biblical home raised me up! I only came to see the heavenly Father's hand on our house after I embraced religion in my middle age. We were His children then, no matter if I had never set foot in His sanctuary. He shaped ours.

So, indeed, what is so profound and novel as a psalm, proverb, or parable becomes a simple expression of human value and goodness. It's no longer an exercise of intellect and wisdom with all its broad implications. Minus all the contemplation, it's just good people being good people. Which, my sister's family was in my eyes.

However, because of our difference of belief at that point, I never spoke of my faith for the sake of our dynamic. I didn't want to make it awkward or to make her uncomfortable. This one night though, I just couldn't take it anymore. I hit this wall inwardly as a silence and lull set in over the phone. I wanted so much to share of my Lord. I had no more to say. I had nothing else to share but Him. I spent so much time thinking of Him and simply being more and more in His love and presence that it felt wrong that I should hide Him—that I would leave Him out of speaking of my day and life. I stammered and got off of the phone. I hadn't even joined a church, and it had been about 6 months of this hibernation honeymoon.

I'd become immersed in Him as most of my friendships and relationships had slowly fallen away from my life in the months preceding my conversion. It was really disturbing at first. What's going on? It was like everyone suddenly fell out of touch. These were people who I saw weekly or every few days. Suddenly, a month would pass without a returned call. I thought I'd become an offense in my changes. I'd put aside using any drugs—tobacco, alcohol, and pot, specifically.

I set down the phone and stared at the knife I was holding over the vegetables. Time seemed to slow down. I felt the Lord saying, *put down the knife.* But dinner? I can't just stop, right? *No, it's ok. Just go for a walk. Any shoes will do, and you don't need keys to lock the door. Just go out.* Ok, so by the end of the sidewalk—to the right or the left, Lord? *To the right.* And just as I turned to go down the sidewalk this dog was running down the street in the same direction.

My neighbor across the street diagonal to me happened to be checking his mail in this moment, too. He shouted, "Is that your dog?" "No," I said, "I think it belongs to my neighbors to the left." So, I ended up chatting with this neighbor I was meeting for the first time after living in that house for over a year and a half. That daily pot habit led to a pretty private life in my suburban setting. Not anymore though. My world opened up—I was free to meet anyone anytime. Freedom.

Turns out he was wearing this shirt with the word "covenant" across it. I knew he was a Christian, and our conversation revealed he was actually a pastor. I felt like a girl in grade school waiting for a boy she liked to ask her out. I had the same inward anxiety: *I hope he asks me to come. I hope he asks me. Please ask.* For all the times I may have ever turned away those evangelists on the UT campus of my undergraduate days, now I was the one praying inside to be invited. Well, he didn't ask. For heaven's sake. Now, I've been around so many beautiful Christians who are this way, being careful to honor others in sharing their faith gently. Nevertheless, I felt blessed by a mini-miracle. Wow.

I just couldn't go on with my sister one more night leaving my Lord in the secret privacy of my existence when He'd become such a beautiful part of my life, and I loved Him. It was as though my sister would purposely hide any talk of her husband just to try to honor my comfort. I couldn't do it anymore. I didn't care. It's just not right. Any comfort zones will just need to bend around my Lord.

So, I got to meet Pastor Joe and walked a couple laps around the block to work out my feelings and thoughts. I came back home and looked up his church online. I decided to go that Sunday. It was the first church I attended since converting. Talk about a blessed day. For all the times I'd ever attended a church as a guest of some friend I had a Saturday night slumber party with as a kid, nothing was like arriving as a lover of the Lord. Before, I'd always felt like an anthropologist, in retrospect. Like, am I supposed to sing? Am I supposed to the do the triangle thingy the Catholic people do? Since both my childhood best friends were Catholic I had this encounter and confusion as a kid sitting in the pews, the guest.

Not this time. I showed up early and nervous, like a kid on the first day of school in a new town, not knowing anyone. My future mentor would eventually baptize me a year later. But, on this day, she saw me sitting alone in the empty sanctuary and invited me to sit with her and her husband. I felt so cared for and relieved someone took note of me. From that point forward, she graciously took me under her wing.

I started going to this church from that point on, amazed at this new reality of having a church family and a place to love God with other people who love Him, too. After so long of hibernating alone, it was a breath of fresh air. Especially when most of my former relationships had ceased and been replaced by this total devotion to the spirit of the Lord at home. Now, a place I could express my love freely and meet with others who felt the same. The irony—I finally lived a transparent life and was learning to enjoy it's freedom; yet, I felt so isolated and suppressed, unable to be open in my love for my King. Now, I found freedom in His sanctuary. Far from any of the fear that opened this book and most certainly free to love.

Immersed in the Spirit

I**N THOSE DAYS,** He felt like an enveloping force of love and pure authority. He was big, strong, firm, and surrounded me with His protective arms. Like a cloak around my being was His presence. I didn't want to be with anyone. I literally didn't want to marry or consider another man in my life. I just wanted Him. Forever.

At one point, I found myself at this conference for women, for believers. An auditorium full of women in love with Jesus. It was amazing. The girl in the row in front of me turned to me, and we sat chatting about our faith. I shared in this tender newness, still so secret and intimate, so inward was every bit of my faith. I was excited too, though.

She and I shared a mutual happiness about being there and about our Lord. She was describing extending an invitation to a girl friend to join her for the event. The girl shied away, reluctant to come to a religious event. She said, "I told her, you've never seen something till you see an auditorium full of women in love with Jesus." I knew what she meant. I was in deep. And this was, indeed, a most beautiful sight!

Even as I sit writing, the song playing right now is by an artist I have loved from those early days. Shawn McDonald is singing: *I must confess that it's true, that I'm nothing without You…cuz without You I feel undone.* Is this man singing to his bride? Perhaps, but everyone of his songs are love songs to the Lord. Falling in love with the Lord is hardly limited to the ladies, is the point of this reflection. And I find that absolutely beautiful. What man would anyone be free to fall in love with but the Beloved? That is how he is referenced in the scripture. The Father's beloved, His chosen one. Like Israel, but the ransom for many. The prophet Isaiah said He was marred beyond the semblance of a man—this was His lot.

Well before I had read such scriptures, in the start of my studies that summer that I commit myself, I would spend the mornings in the book of Luke. Initially, I would go through my day following my morning Luke study giving thought to God, but only occasionally. Since it was summer break, I'd spend a couple of hours studying. Later, I'd give thought to the lessons I'd learned in the morning. This one day I was shopping at a thrift store in town and got a random surprise of a call from a student teacher I had mentored for some time the previous year. I really liked this girl. She was full of zeal for teaching and for art. She took the initiative to do everything I'd ask and more. She was pure potential.

Given my esteem for her, I was happy to hear from her at all, much less to hear that she'd gotten engaged. Wow! Wonderful news. Well, it just so happened as I was checking out at the register, the attendant asked me, "Do you have any good news to share today? If you do, we will give you a 50% discount." Wow! Again, how lovely. I like a discount. So, I said, "You know, I actually just got really good news." I told her about my story. She looked disappointed. What (?) is going on. Why? My heart fell. I couldn't understand where I went wrong. She didn't say anything. She just finished ringing me up, and I left the store confused and down.

I called up my phone friend from Louisiana. She was my help in this change I was undergoing. She had been sharing her faith transformation with me for the last year. She comforted me—"Oh," she said, "she probably wanted you to say something about the Lord." Ohhhh. My. Well then. I failed. My friend assured me, "You're ok, you didn't fail. Don't worry. You're perfect as you are. She is how she is, and you are as you need to be." I felt comforted and came away from that incident meditating on this.

I got to a place eventually when I thought of the Lord all day and wouldn't imagine life any differently, ever again. I couldn't relate to this woman yet, though. She had hoped for a mutually shared praise of her King, and all I had to offer was some news. There is nothing like praising God for his works on any given day, especially in the shared love of another believer. This was an openly Christian thrift store. So I learned this lesson over time as I came to consider Him more and more through any given day.

There was a time the previous fall, for example, when this same friend would share the occasional scripture or praise song with me through email.

I'd read and listen and wonder about this strange music. My music then was rather "worldly" as Christians would say. It was alternative, electronic, and underground type of music. I suppose it was created or listened to at least part of time while under the influence of some sort mind-altering something or other whether alcohol or pot at the least.

When she had stayed with me a few days the previous summer, I recall she couldn't handle hearing this music playing. Her spirit was already sensitive in advance of her conscious transformation later that fall. I remember sitting in the car with her helping her figure out why she was suffering all these health problems. She said, "I think this is about God." Well, in my atheism, I thought, psshah, God. Huh. Well, by that fall she was the one praying for me, going through the existential pits of my one-third life crisis. It *was* about God.

I called her one night this fall before my conversion after I couldn't sleep for several days. Literal all night insomnia with an urgency about my being—must clean and set things in proper order now. Then, I'd be trying to sleep and be overwhelmed with these "memory movies" running endlessly through my mind. They were playing back to me shameful and embarrassing moments in my life—in the classroom, with friends, in my relationships. I was sooo not the person I thought I was in my much more pleasant self perception.

This turned out to be the blind ideal I was aiming for so valiantly while I just turned an eye towards the good and neglected to take note of my utter hypocrisies. Well, that was a mental beating that was rather terrifying at the time. So much more obvious and banal in the retelling. Very intense as it took place. So I confided again in this friend, and she said something that struck me through. I was so self-conscious from these reflections going through my head. I felt utterly critical and ashamed. She said, "You are not your own judge. Only God is the judge, and He may not judge you as harshly as you judge yourself."

Well, that was news at the time. First off, I wasn't even thinking of God. In fact, I hadn't given thought to God in a long time. Not as a person anyway. So, the first thing that statement pierced was the chasm of time between me and my childhood, whenever it was that I had lost touch with the fatherly friend of mine I used to spend hours playing with as a child. I began to fathom Him and wondered what He might possibly think of all this failure I apparently covered up with lies about how delightful and successful I was. Noooo. I never needed to know anyway; yet, I was grateful nonetheless to be informed. To wake up is better than to continue to go about in the same ignorance. So it had it's upside, but man was it a bitter pill.

To imagine God might actually view me with a desire to help me, that these things were being revealed to me through Him for the purpose of waking me up and not judging me finally—what a relief! It was comforting to realize He didn't view me as horrifically as I felt. And then, that He'd want my well being and would work to that end was even greater a hope than waking up would have been in and of itself. So, in the end, with my friend's counsel, I came through that bout whole. Ultimately, it was a part of the jostling my life was enduring in preparation for the Lord's revelation the next spring.

This is the season my relationships began mysteriously falling away. Later I would learn such terms as "pruning" being a part of the Gardener's work in a person's life or soul. Well, my life got some major pruning in preparation for the commitment to come. Slowly but surely, I began having more and more spiritual experiences that I couldn't credit to an altered state of mind. I was, for example, a regular curser—a sailor mouth, if you will, outside of school. Part of that happy hour life. Adult stuff. There was a bit of nudge nudge, wink wink at school with the kids. No, you can't curse in class. Pretend you're at the bank. Would you curse there? Then, you can't curse here. In other words, save it for your own time and space cuz I'm not having it in my room. Besides, if I don't get to curse, then neither do you.

Well, in the course of another phone call with my friend the following spring, I was apparently piercing her being with my curse words. How would I ever come to know these words do such a thing? Because out of nowhere it started happening to me this one afternoon at our usual Friday afternoon happy hour patio. The normal flow of open conversations and two dollar cocktails turned into a battlefield as each curse word hit my sensitized frame with impact. I couldn't handle it. They were like bullets. I left early and headed home. Stopped going altogether. In another instance, I'm chatting with my friend on the phone and she's angry at rush hour traffic. I had to pull the phone away from my ear it was so painful to hear the curse words.

Furthermore, the use of the words just fell from my mouth. No effort to stop—they just never came out again. Bizarre. I shared this new phenomena with my friend after a few solid weeks of this new physical rejection of cursing. She asked when it began, and I told her, "Well, about a few weeks ago, I guess." She said, "Oh, well, I have to confess something to you. It was really hard to hear you talking using them so much so I prayed to God about it, right about a few weeks ago." She had never made any mention to me.

She did exactly what a Christian ought to, incidentally. Without even correcting me, she simply took her concern to the King. Well, the King took care of the matter Himself. No need to rebuke me. I got the point and the transformation. Never mind that I began to realize the power of God supernaturally. Way stronger than anything I'd ever used to push the boundaries of my own consciousness.

This was in the spring when I'd begun having strong intuitions about a lot of things. Put away pot. Stop drinking. Be friends with the man you've been dating for the last year. Give the intimacy a rest and simply be together as people until you know more about the true commitment potential between you two. And so on. Steps towards sanctity. Some word I had never used before and consider all the time now.

My friends began to notice and comment—you sure are bolder than usual. Some of them pulled away. I was speaking my mind more, standing in my truth. Rather than apologizing and letting others joke or put me down or dismiss me and so on, I'd stand up for my thoughts and beliefs. I had a stronger sense of self, more assertive than the passive people-pleaser I had been accustomed to being in my personality's coping mechanisms. I started to receive the occasional spiritual guidance from angels as I'd journal in that season. One stated, *You must reclaim your power.* Well, this was an entirely novel concept to me at the time. I couldn't understand it really, even though I can now see that's what I was doing more and more. It didn't necessarily go over well as I rocked the boat of our norms.

So, I fell away from the bar and ended up spending quite a bit of time alone. I was used to seeking companionship—avoiding spending time alone like the plague. I didn't like it none. Too much silence and anxiety. Loneliness. Nevertheless, I started spending whole weekends in the solitary din of my own company. Over time, I discovered—I actually like myself. Strange. I just never made a point of pushing through the first few of such weekends to see what might live on the other side of simply experiencing it.

It just so happened all this time to myself unfolded alongside a growing relationship with God. Go figure. He would occupy alone time. Who knows you better than God? Never mind being your Maker, but being the consciousness ever aware of all the layers of one's lived existence—well, heavens, He's just gonna be an expert on every intimate aspect of one's being. And so, He became my companion over time. Slowly, the spring became summer, and by fall, I realized His spirit was healing my inner wounds.

I had no idea how much loneliness I carried about under all that rushing around. So much insecurity. So much tension. All this energy seeking the next outlet, the next relief and peace with someone or some hit, or some sip or search through some book or movie or what have you. Always on the go, on the take. Gotta fill the bottomless pit of my existence ever covering the emptiness that apparently longed for Him.

I had heard of such things. A God-shaped hole in the heart or soul. Now I knew it to be the absolute truth of my haste. Quickly, before I'm left with it again. That nameless thing. The invisible race. Slowly, but surely, I began to hear His voice more and more. Less was His presence a direct and powerful sense of intuition, and more so was it His actual words being conveyed to my mind in a particular tone I knew was Him.

It was not the angel guides, male or female as they are. He would help me, for example, when I had questions while studying scripture and seeking understanding. My questions would arise naturally, and as I jotted them down, I might just hear some guidance to help me reach for the answer. I felt amazed at this form of communication. Why would He commune with me? For some reason, I imagined this limitless God like some kind of cosmic CEO who's too busy to spend time with me. Who would I be to speak to directly? Nobody. So, initially I was rather shocked. Then I began to adapt. Then I grew attached.

By the fall term of teaching high school my fourth year, I would get home in the afternoons and immediately sit down to the kitchen table I conducted my studies at and seek Him in our time together. I wanted Him more and more. Time with Him. I wanted so much to learn His wisdom and way. The gospel of Luke was finished by August, and I had moved on to the next and to reading epistles by winter.

I was taken and absorbed by the wisdom of the scriptures. What sort of writing was this? For all my studies and for all the critical theory and comprehensive exams and thesis writing my two masters degrees in liberal arts demanded, I had never read anything like this. I left grad school with a head full of intellectual seas rocking the waves of my mental capacity to their boundaries. I put away reading altogether until I started the Bible. And nothing I had enjoyed immersing my mind in as much as I did the literature I consumed in grad school even began to compare to what I was exposed to in this new endeavor to learn about my God.

One or two paragraphs would take me a couple of days minimum to journal and digest, so rich was the material. I was in love, not only with my Lord, but also with the scriptures. I never seemed to exhaust the hunger to learn more. I began memorizing them eventually so that I should have them with me in the event I couldn't actually open a Bible to feed myself, like when I was driving or standing in line at the grocery or something. I had to have them ever on my mind, before my sight. It was like a way to be with Him between my encounters with His spirit at the times He would come to commune with me.

On top of this love affair with His Word and wisdom, I began noticing other aspects of the transformation taking place in my person. From the day I commit myself in that kitchen, from the very moment my confession was complete, I literally experienced an altered state of reality and felt this peace and powerfully shifted sense of perspective overwhelm my being. I looked about the kitchen and realized, if He has died for me, then I must guard my life because it's worth His life.

I started to clean out my house. I dumped half-gallon bargain bottles of liquor down the drain. I threw this foot-and-a-half tall hookah into the garbage in my garage. Out it went, into the trash—along with all the flavored tubs of expensive tobacco and all those rolls of coals that lit the countless daily hours of fruity, curling smoke. This habit was another financial investment, and many of my days involved at least a few bowls I might have smoked alone or with a friend.

I hit my bookshelf next, sifting through the spines and plucking out titles that seemed suspect. So much literature that ever struck my efforts at intelligence and self development as being so sophisticated. Perusing the pages, I realized—this stuff is dark and not of the light. The scales had fallen from my eyes, just as the saying goes. I piled a good chunk of my books into the trash. And then the confusion—some weren't so clear cut and I was left with a decision to make. Anyway. I headed out to buy my first Bible that morning, driving with this bizarrely thick peace about everything.

As I walked into my favorite bookstore, I wondered of translations and vaguely realized there's a lot of controversy about this sort of stuff, right? How will I know which one to choose? Well, He will guide me! Duh. And sure enough, I found my baby since then, my hippie Bible, as I refer to it. It wasn't stuffy at all. It was bound in a sackcloth-beige canvas. Furthermore, it had a green tree of life stamped on the cover. It was called "The Green Bible," as the passages dealing with the stewardship of creation were highlighted throughout the text in green. This NRSV version was dedicated to concern for creation in light of the current environmental crisis facing the earth and its people.

After getting home, I cracked it open and the middle left me at the mercy of some rather daunting parts of the prophet Isaiah. Heavens. Talk about scary. I shut it quickly. Not starting there. No way. That's when I settled on the book of Luke, deciding I'd start in the New Testament to learn about this Jesus I commit myself to that morning.

By the rest of that week, I realized He had delivered me from every attachment I had—alcohol, tobacco, and even coffee. I simply felt no longing or desire anymore. I felt free. I even had greater and clearer energy than I ever had relying on coffee for so many years. I was amazed. And grateful. Soon enough, He began to show me how much of my life and person were being squandered in trying to control and self-regulate all this minutiae of decisions about this and that which required constant modification to be an adequate or better and better person. Wow. I had no idea how much time and attention was devoted to these little decisions. How much cream in my coffee? What kind of creamer? Not too much sugar now. That's bad. Good heavens.

He introduced me to a powerful insight about health. Emotions are extremely strong in their effect on physiology. All that control and anxiety is actually worse for your health than the poisons one aims to regulate. Oh. Well, duh. Just free yourself up, and be moderate without abusing things. Makes sense. How liberating! Needless to say, by that fall, I became completely immersed in the Spirit. Apart from afternoon and evening study sessions, I began increasingly to listen to worship music and my heart grew intense towards the Lord. I would awake and worship, worship by night cooking or what not—didn't matter. I'd be in a heap of worship some way or other. Lost in Him.

My heart had changed. I would cry with ease, when I didn't cry all my life—like a man I was. I went from hating pink to loving pink, from giving hardened thought at best to the prospect and idea of marriage and children to loving pregnant women something fierce. I had a radar for pregnant women. I'd sense one literally from across a large room in a crowd from behind my view. I'd turn, and what do you know? A pregnant woman!

And the joy and delight they inspired in my person—absolutely bizarre, and *not* me. I decided, Jesus really, really, really loves mothers-to-be. Heavens. All I wanted to do was go gush on them about how absolutely beautiful they were and congratulations and don't you worry, God loves you and you're gonna be alright and so on. It was potent.

I couldn't be in a remotely loud room without feeling blasted by the sound waves. It was like a shock to my entire being. I was so utterly sensitive. I noticed my wounds would heal in no time, compared to before. I was a whole new person, a new creation as the scripture states in the letter of St. Paul to the church of the Corinthians. *So if anyone is in Christ, there is a new creation: everything old has passed away; see, everything has become new! 2 Cor 5:17*

This one evening late in October, with winter just around the bend, I was preparing dinner when it seemed the Lord wanted to have a hand at cooking through me. I felt guided to prepare a meal with spices I'd never use and in a manner so picture perfect and beautiful that the meal was most definitely not my doing. I would usually throw stuff together on the fly while trying to remember to turn down the heat so I wouldn't burn the pan again. When it was said and done, my meals typically had a heap of stir fried veggies over a bed of pasta or with a chunk of olive bread or something. Simple enough.

Not His meal. He decided to season a half of an acorn squash like a Better Homes and Gardens cover design or something. With a couple other portions alongside, this meal faced me at the dinner table when it was complete like He'd served me personally at His own table—His princess He was treating to a fancy dinner. I felt absolutely loved and precious and special. I'd never felt quite so much that way in my life. As if all that wasn't enough, I could sense His being sitting across from me.

As I sat there eating this food I'd never have come up with, I realized each flavor appealed to my sense of taste in a completely novel way I enjoyed a lot and precisely. I began to imagine the measure of His omniscient knowledge and wisdom. I felt so special. I was overwhelmed. Suddenly the whole of my former wayward life came down upon me, confronted with His love. They say, the kindness of the Lord brings one to repentance. Well, my repentant heart just sank to the floor. My spirit literally crashed downward. I felt dizzy with its fall. I sensed in my being the emotion of regret so strongly. But alongside this, I felt that familiar sense of rebuke and correction I had grown accustomed to by then. Regret was a sin, somehow, too.

Well, that was just too much. I ended up lost that night in an ocean of murky black sitting on the kitchen floor. I'd fall in and out of consciousness at various turns coming through a deep and thick black haze of yuck and unconsciousness. I made it to bed at some point and woke up again to stand and rebuke dark spirits with speech I'd never even used before guiding me through the battle. By morning, I gingerly stepped outside on the back patio and sensed whom I would now account was Father God showing me, *See, it is all still here*—the new day, fresh with it's life. The yard full of it's grass overgrown with little flowers that were likely deemed weeds, a beautiful negligence. He seemed to be saying, *You are loved. Don't allow hell to consume you for your sins of old.*

I've been trying to wrap my mind around this reality ever since. In all the torment and suffering I've endured for the last six of these seven years, I've yet to fully grasp this lesson shown me so early on. When I consider it, regret is an emotion I would know and feel. None of my sin was lost on the Lord when He chose to reveal His reality to me at that point in my life's path. Nothing is lost on Him.

If He had any doubts about whether or not to show me grace, forgiveness, and wisdom through faith, then He could abide in His own sovereign choice to remain hidden from me as He had all those years. But, indeed, He chose otherwise, and I imagine, He has no regrets in Himself. Nor does my regret serve my being in Him. This may be easily stated and understood as a concept, but living it's reality has proven to me to be a challenge. He is so good. And it's so easy to feel unworthy. As this whole book began.

Then the Darkness Came

FROM AROUND THIS time forward, about seven or eight months into this new faith walk, I began experiencing night attacks. Apart from the nightmares, that first night was not the only one in which I had to arise and rebuke spirits. Holy Spirit gave me the words to speak. I was hardly versed in the common Christian topic of spiritual warfare. As I'd come to learn more of this over time, my experiences were hardly unique.

Alongside this new and challenging dilemma, one day I began realizing my health had been suffering more than I had really taken note. I arose from this chair, lost in the scriptures, and became really dizzy, yet again. This was a normal occurrence by then through any given day along with the sensation of heart palpitations at random. Also, from that spring I'd begun experiencing these odd days of pain. For three days or so I'd be struck with sudden aches and pains like a flu but without the fever and other symptoms, wiped out and writhing around on my couch wondering what on earth was going on. These bouts were somewhat frequent in time, and I just got used to them and decided they must be spiritual in nature since I found no physical source.

On top of all this, I was so lost in the Spirit my appetite fell away as I spent more and more time in scripture and communion. From that conversion onward I experienced a reduced appetite. I began slimming down, which was nice initially. By this time though, I'd gotten super skinny. Not since high school was I at this weight that wasn't entirely off for a 5 foot 1 person, but I freaked out a bit this one morning I weighed in at 94 pounds with no effort to lose from the original 130 or so that I weighed before.

That morning I broke down crying as I confessed my concerns to two of my art teaching mentors at school. They had already approached me about my changes. Kathy, knowing my past and history with eating disorders had asked me about anorexia, and I told her I was making no effort to lose and had no stake in the changes; but rather, I was at their mercy.

Well, before I knew it I had made an appointment with my physician for noon that day suddenly overwhelmed with the sense that I may have neglected a serious situation going on that needed to be addressed soon. My assistant principal and the school principal I loved so much called me into a meeting to make way for my leave which became a two month leave of absence. I prepared my classes for my extended departure and left that day.

Kathy, the fine arts chair and my dear friend, was not surprised at this turn of events. This took place in mid-December. The month of November was probably one of the most radical and intense months of my life. I had begun creating art "under the influence" of the Spirit's great power. I spent time in class faint and dizzy with His omniscience in utter awe of what was being accomplished through my being.

We were working on collage, and I'd typically work on my own collages alongside the kids. While I had always loved this particular practice especially and felt it came unusually naturally and even intuitively to me, these collages I had begun experiencing were entirely different. The scraps of random images and colors and textures would come together in truly uncanny arrangements. They were topped with words and messages that were all scriptural wisdom beyond my knowledge.

My experience of His power allowed me to understand His exact and precise mastery of every iota of space and time. I'd lose some teeny piece of typed word like "the" on the floor. Mind you, the scrap of paper was smaller than my finger tip could barely glue properly; yet, I'd reach down and retrieve it immediately from a pile of trash scraps, my eyes and hand directed to it's minuscule presence. One collage that was particularly packed with meaning took the course of a whole school day to create and left me exhausted and dizzy with His presence.

I would spend my conference periods holed up in my office, communing and reading scripture and writing His counsel and wisdom. At times, my ignorance of holiness would transgress His being so deeply I was overwhelmed with disdain and rejection and fear. I'd then be lost in lengthy prayers of repentant apology and pleas for forgiveness. Now, far from this measure of sensitivity and immersion, I realize I was truly communing so powerfully then that I would transgress pure holiness. As if I knew of Isaiah's plea for clean lips! This prophet had to have his lips touched with a hot coal to be prepared for his calling. To prophesy in the name of the One who sits on a throne, untouchably perfect in justice, is no small assignment!

Sometimes this would go on for hours from the end of the school day into the night sitting in that little lamp lit closet-office. Those collages especially—were their messages of God or the devil? Being so new to the scriptures and the wisdom of faith, I just couldn't tell sometimes. One was so potent and confusing, I tore it in four and then retrieved it from the trash in a later fit of regret and re-taped it back together. I was overwhelmed with the gravity of the task of discernment steeped so deeply in the Spirit.

Filling notebooks with scriptural reflections was nothing too unusual, but soon I was transcribing knowledge beyond my being. I drew diagrams and illustrations of the knowledge of God I would later come to realize were actually accurate. One such drawing described the seven spirits of the new man in Christ. Well, that later proved to be true.

I wondered at the time of this knowledge. What on earth was I doing? Holy schmoly. Hardly a technical term, but why me? Why would all this be entrusted to me? I developed a deep sense of gravity about the call on my life. I was warned my purpose was to help unite man under the cross of Christ. That I had a divine destiny and a part of my purpose was to impart a message to people that was uniquely mine. My parents were rather taken aback by these declarations, as was my sister at our ground breaking breakfast one morning. I had been instructed to share this news to prepare them. And it would require preparation for the measure of power I was shortly stewarding.

For example, I had been invited at that time to join this planning team the new superintendent had organized to chart the guiding vision and objectives of the district with the help of school and community members. I can remember sitting in on these meetings with a mind so strong and powerfully prophetic in analytic capacity that it would struggle to keep pace with other people and the discussion at hand. This intelligence scoped broadly with branched precision while reaching yet into future concerns.

Much of my thinking proved accurate and relevant, true for all it's bizarre power. I had to tailor my comments to reflect a humble participation with the group. I didn't always succeed and felt the familiar sense of rebuke for failing my call to humility. Well, for heaven's sake, it was no small gift I was suddenly stewarding. I wondered what on earth all this was for?

I had accepted this change as much as I was able to bear it stably. Then, I had this turn of anxiety over a legitimate health issue that got a bit blown out of proportion in my response to its scary ambiguity. Since it involved my heart palpitating and and purring randomly, I freaked out and ended up on hiatus from work for a time searching out medical help. In this season of healing at home, I spent a good deal of time once again immersed in the Spirit helping me get better through remedies I would never know to create. I loved the Lord. I wanted to marry Him alone.

I'd browse my closet in the morning and sense His preference. I simply felt loved through the days. For all the stress of the dark, I felt grateful ultimately. The house and days were littered with signs of His presence and love. One night, I sat on the kitchen floor eating as though I was with my soul mate. Not the slightest hint of guilt or judgment. I could sense him sitting with me. I was absolutely in love. Pure quiet, intimate joy.

Like my best friend in all of ever is the truth of His being. This is surely the Truth. Likely, I'd imagine, for so many souls. He is my origin. Of this I am sure. I came from Him some time and place ago, before I was a material person, incarnate in this humanity I've lived for so long now I can't imagine dying as it sinks in more and more approaching my fortieth birthday this year. I used to consider it intellectually or contemplatively. I believe in heaven and most certainly hope on it, even in the face of my deepest doubts and surrender to the righteous Judge, beset as I may be by my legitimate failures. Nonetheless, the fathoming of what that means, the transition spiritually, is so well beyond my mind. I know this much: I hope I return to my source, to Him.

This time allowed me to heal for the most part. I received warnings, as I faced my ultimate shame and failure with the whole affair, that my true fall from grace had yet to come and would be so painful that I would need His love in my heart to survive it. At points my immersion in the mystical became so intense I experienced "truths" that were every bit real in my experience even if they weren't necessarily relevant to reality as I lived it in the world.

Among my beliefs in all this: that Jesus truly was my one and only soul mate, like my actual true husband. Like a man would be. Just happens to be the Alpha and Omega of reality. No biggie. I suppose it's the calling of a sister in a convent, a comfort though it's hardly my calling. I mean I've since read a bazillion near death experience accounts. One involved a man sitting on a rock with Him in the cosmos as he received counsel for his return. Again, no biggie. Just a talk with the King. He's so humble He's got time and sits with such as us. The goal was to show him his place in what was happening. Life was so painful for him then, mercy stepped in to help him understand and find the courage to come through.

Pieces Coming Together

I SPENT THOSE NEXT two months at home mostly, making art, reading the Bible, and seeing the occasional specialist to check out my heart. By the time I finally got in for an echocardiogram, my heart symptoms were already slowly healing. Frustrating, but a welcomed relief nonetheless. I never did get any proof anything was wrong for as bad as I looked and felt. So it goes.

I did try to take this course I saw at church called "Perspectives" about God and his plan for the diverse cultures of the world. At the time, I was rather amazed that I, an Iranian, could be a Christian also—revealing my ignorance of what it really means to be Christian, of course. I suppose I'd imagined they were all white for some reason. Growing up in Texas maybe. Well, there's Christians of every stripe because God is everyone's God, and who doesn't need a Savior when He is Just? I had curiosity then, being a social justice activist sort of art teacher, given my time in applied anthropology and all that critical theory. Yup, I could go on about "hegemony" but had never used the word "salvation."

I was rather impressed initially: words like grace, testimony, and salvation were totally new to my vocabulary and speech. The word grace came to be my way of referencing the supernatural stuff God was doing in my life, not the actual meaning of grace towards sin, as in, forgiveness and clemency. Nope, still hadn't got it right. In fact, the cross itself was a strange mystery. This much was not—I hated it. I wished it never was. Nor was it right that my Jesus ever had to suffer it. Well, that's kind of the point girl! Didn't get that. I was frustrated of it's existence and that stupid one on the stage at church annoyed me. Why? It is the symbol of our redemption and His generosity towards men.

Of course, but not You, me. I wanted it to be me! Like I'd have it in me to suffer even a fraction of what He ever endured. Yet still, it was simply wrong, and I had this antagonism towards the Father on this account for years. Like, this is somehow all His fault. I didn't like Him. My Jesus! He's no one's Son, just my Jesus, you see. Done and done.

Never mind that it was also just a bit hard to fix my attention on any other Gods but for my Love. There's two more. You can't leave them out. I always sensed I was looked at by the three of them as a bit lazy and inappropriately partial in my feelings for the Son. I didn't care. Just one focus for the heart. My favorite psalm and first memorized scripture was Psalm 86:11—*Teach me Your way, O Lord, that I may walk in Your truth. Give me an undivided heart to revere Your name.* This was my hope. An undivided heart. Not three ways.

So this Perspectives class was intense and after several weeks, I realized, *Oh, this is to prepare missionaries! Oops.* I was so not preparing for missions and could barely keep up, so I bowed out of the effort. As for the next undertaking, I booked a weekend conference in Portland after seeing a poster at church about God's plan for social justice. It was called "The Justice Conference." Well, that sounds great! What an exciting novelty to activist me that God liked the same stuff I did. What does Jesus have to do with Justice? Truly. I was that innocent. With a master's degree or two. It's just a little amusing to me now. He is everything to do with justice. He *is* Justice. The whole of the Bible is historical justice through the lens of God's relationship to a particular portion of all humanity He chose to single out as "His own."

It's not like the scriptures don't claim Him as God of all or exhibit the same justice and preference for any who pursue the way of purity and righteousness. The way of justice. He is the Judge. That's the whole point of fearing the Lord, goofball. In fact, I spent the morning just today reading the book of Amos and thought to myself, heavens, talk about fear of the Lord. The proclamations were stiff. You wouldn't want to be around for the decrees of this man. He was run out of town so heinous was the forthcoming declaration of judgment.

This weekend in Portland was, however, for a naive and love immersed new creation in Christ to discover an attraction to sessions about economics and to meet a friend by the leading of the Holy Spirit for the first time. At the time, I was skipping even more sessions in favor of reading the book of Acts in this little coffeeshop. I like cozy and reading, so I had chosen this one stool in front of a window wall overlooking the session space, tucked into the corner of the shop. I kept feeling distracted from this one section about the apostle Peter healing the lame man by the entrance of the temple. I looked up several times just to eye the same woman at one of these tables.

Stop looking, that's bad. She'll notice—really, stop. Well, soon enough I saw her get up and exit the frame of my view. Then, next thing I know she's walking up to me. She asked if I needed any help with what I was reading. I explained the passage and my question to her. She confessed the Holy Spirit led her to meet me. I was amazed.

I thought there was something strange about the way she walked off. Like she was lost inwardly. I imagined I look this way when I'm being guided in the Spirit. Sure enough it was true. Well, how absolutely precious. As we exchanged about our interests, it came up that she, too, was from Dallas, teaching economics at a university there. I confessed that I felt oddly attracted to all the sessions about economics and that I was an art teacher. Well, she was looking for an artist to help her with a t-shirt design she was considering.

It was a match! The weekend was filled with such as this. I was continually amazed at the work of the Spirit. While I only attended four sessions, I met many souls from around the world. One man was from Cambodia. His story was neat because he actually threw his first Bible away—down the river it went while he rode a train to the next town. He said he was determined not to disrespect his father's tradition and heritage with this new belief and religion. That didn't last because, in time, he came to accept Christ and now cherished his Bible, and the Lord. He was there to serve Him.

At the time, this type of story was new to me. I never had such a conflict in my faith story. Since then, though, I have come to see this story again and again—t he severing of ties with tradition while yet maintaining respect for ancestors. This essential issue is at the root of so much conflict and violence, especially in more traditional cultures not so modernized throughout the world. With regularity, news outlets and prayer chains air the needs of children accepting the Lord at the mercy of parents so angry at their child's conversion that they are a threat to their very life. Children often must escape to a community and church severing familial ties just to continue in their faith safely.

I realized that I don't always consider the benefits of living in a prosperous nation and culture of relative peace and diversity. I know that I have no idea what I have and what I've lived, just to read of these souls' stories in the news. But the beauty of God is just this: His people's story is endlessly multifaceted. Each facet a face and story with it of devotion and transformation by His work and Spirit. Each story unique and precious in its own right.

By the time I made it back to school after this leave, I was faced with this landscape of absence and rumors and an awkward return to the stage of art instruction. I may have been restored of health relatively speaking, but I now entered into that season of torment by the entities that showered barbs of sexual denigration on me for all my former sexual history. No aspect of my past justified the torments I endured. I understood it to be the berating of the enemy, the devil, because I was warned that he had "taken note of my faith."

None of this made it any easier to endure. And, none of this mattered in the scheme of my hopes in Christ. The hope of being with the Lord one day was worth any pain and suffering to me. I would simply hold onto my God to get through most days. And the days were exhausting. I'd get home some afternoons only to wake up some hour of the night on the couch I remembered sitting on briefly right after getting home.

Eventually, I discovered that waking up at 3 or 4 am meant God wanted me to attend some matter—there was work to do before the work day. Once I caught on, rather than trying to force sleep again, I was so much better off for it. Inevitably, I had energy for the day, too. I also discovered that if I just spent even the first two hours before school listening to music loving Him and reading Bible, the days were charged with greater strength and energy than others.

I made the connection to my morning practice one afternoon walking to my car especially peppy given the day. Feeling enough energy, in fact, to just head on over to a coffeeshop and keep reading the book of Isaiah I had begun and found myself pleasantly immersed within. It's hardly a pleasant text. It's terrifying. Yet, the verses came alive in me, unfolding in complex and amazing relation to the New Testament verses I had memorized more and more. It was all so connected! And this connectivity made these studies crackle with understanding and awe for me. No book was ever like this in all my nerdy life.

I finished out the spring term successfully with the tremendous support and care of my coworkers and supervisors, as well as my fans among the students. In all my quirky eccentricities and shortcomings, I seemed to somehow attract a faithful group of supporting students among the larger group of this school of 3000 plus ninth through twelfth graders.

By fall, things really seemed to come together as I discovered I'd been blessed to receive one of the grants I'd submit to our principal, conceived in one of those early mornings. I was now charged with starting a novel AP art class modeled after anthropology research and aiming to expose students to a community service opportunity to be professionals in school! The vision was lovely, but enacting this was another story as the term unfolded a road of trial and temptation I never even noticed until each one had managed to succeed my ignorance of such things. Sadly, I never gave thought to the word "temptation" until the following year. Yup.

That's pretty bad for a scripture obsessed girl memorizing such words as, "Let us then be alert and sober, children of the day as the night is passing and the light has shone upon us, chosen in the beloved for grace" and on and on. Duh. Watch out for that prowling lion, the devil, seeking anyone to devour already! But no, I chose instead to give in to the opportunity to date that handsome, young blond man that seemed so familiar the third time he walked by my table in a month. This one day studying Bible after church on a Sunday at one of my favorite coffeeshops, he not only walked in, but then happened to choose the table to my right to sit and break out his Bible, too. Eventually, after some "random" glancing about landed our gaze in a mutual curiosity upon each other a handful of times, we ended up in confession.

This sense of familiarity he had to me, as if I had already met him or knew him somehow, was apparently mutual. The coincidence! As it was, I was left to wonder, but now it's been clarified. Indeed, we'd never met, yet we both had this same sense of the other. It went something like this— Me: "So, I'm working on this idea to make movies about God's work in Denton." Him: "Woah, I love photography and I've been meaning to learn. I just got a nice camera. Can you teach me?"

He was of a kind and gentle disposition. Over time, he revealed his character and personality to be one of the most encouraging, loving, and uplifting souls I'd come across. He was just a really good guy. We hit it off right away, and discovered a common bond that led us into encounters that bloomed into a friendship. What began as "photography lessons," eventually, turned into his confronting me one night: "I care about you and think of you a lot. Do you feel the same?" Yes, I've been thinking of you quite a bit, too. I feel this care for your well being, more than I usually care for a friend. "Would you be open to dating?" Yes, I think I would like that. And so, over this one dinner, our friendship became more, officially. Now, out of nowhere, after a lapse in any romantic relationship that had involved falling in love with God, I found myself soothed from all the stress I knew in any torments I'd struggled. I drank up our hand holding and the tremendous comfort of being hugged and held like a thirsty wanderer.

I had forgotten these comforts and most certainly had a new sense of relating, having left those "worldly" ways behind for a devoted effort to please God in my life. Does praying daily for His guidance in honoring this beautiful soul and our relationship translate into success in this regard? Not necessarily. What had been a private sense of sanctuary in my being and my heart suddenly made way for a new family member to come in. Errick and I both agreed our hope and goal was to discern in this effort whether we were right for marriage. So, essentially, I had this new potential husband in my life.

I met this young man the fall of the school term I had begun that graced me with that grant from the district. Talk about distracted. Furthermore, we both drank alcohol. I had begun drinking wine and beer again after I had spent the first 8 months of my salvation clean of even coffee. I began again, of all things, after facing some pressure in my friend and family relations about my suddenly straight edge life.

Initially, I grew hardened and proud in my abstinence—self-righteous. Then, this sin was tempered with a new resolve to reinitiate drinking like those people that have no attachment and never lose their sobriety, seeking no buzz. Well, this was an impossibility for me, apparently. I guess I was the type of person with the tendency to get attached even if I was not abusing it. I knew to put away anything harmful and most especially addicting the first day of committing. I regretted this transition later as I put alcohol away and picked it up and put it away, repeatedly dealing with the same attachment over the next several years.

I can still remember the first time I drank just a bit more than I should have, so that my body and mind were not entirely sober, and after so long. His Spirit lived in me so powerfully then. In this first incident, I was overcome with a distinct and strong sense of *pure infidelity* towards Him. I collapsed on my little couch into this deep depression, unable to escape the effects, but instead forced to ride them out inwardly as I apologized over and over again to His presence.

I was a cheat to give away my sobriety in the slightest. Why be other than true when you're spending time with the friend you love most, who is not sharing your drinks with you and has no need or desire of such things—His company being an *absolute gift* just as it is? But, even after this horrible error, I did it yet again despite the experience. Each time I crossed that line which occurred with even a bit more than a single glass of wine, I grew less and less sensitive in my body and spirit. I rarely drink at all anymore, but I've never regained the sensitivity I once knew.

Back then, by the time I was dating this young man, we spent the evenings wining and dining as people do when they date, especially early on. I should-have, could-have been working on school, but got caught up in my new love affair and its heady beginnings. I was kicking myself by the end of that school year the next spring, after we'd broken up our six month relationship deciding we weren't meant for each other. Man. Now I was left with the fruits of my choices having endured a serious effort to pull my work together in the face of my personal life. Furthermore, the care I'd watched blossoming between he and my best girl friend throughout our relationship, that I sensed was growing softer and deeper, became their new relationship and dating shortly after we had broken up.

Knife to my heart! Not that! It's not like I didn't care for both of them and want their best. I did. But, boy was I wounded for some reason. Our break up had been hard enough as it was, and now this. I was lucky I did as well as I did, in reality, when it came to school. Very emotionally trying season. Ah, the twists and turns of love. What had happened to marrying only my Savior? Well, there was this whole issue of obedience to God's will.

So, early on, after making that choice for myself, I felt conflict from God's perspective—like, are you sure about this, because I may have it in mind to place you in a marriage and even bless you with children. I resisted this notion, but was so eager to be obedient I was also open to it. For all the relationships in my past that never actually worked out, I had fallen in love each time. I left each long term relationship of at least a year or two loving that person yet still. Sometimes, they were difficult bonds to break that required years worth of effort down the line just to sever the heart ties completely. So, my reasoning was—*You know I have no trouble loving and caring for someone, Lord.* I like partnership. So, this wasn't the issue. The real issue was the matter of a split heart. I had wanted to focus mine on Him. Then again, by the time you pick up drinking again, I'd already begun straying in my life.

Ultimately, I ran into so many administrative discoveries, I realized soon enough my morphing class vision wasn't going to actually make. For starters, I should have pursued the technical addition of a service learning course to the curricular offerings at the head of the year as there was no such course offered at all at that point, and the administrative process to modify the course offerings in such a way was somewhat involved.

Next, I would need at least 15 students committed to signing up for it before the course could be added to the offerings. Well, I advertised my concept and had about 8 devoted students which simply wasn't sufficient for it to actually become a reality. In all my efforts to adapt the model to the shifting circumstances, the course had transformed into a different vision altogether in a sense. It was to be a class about "Self," which strangely was the entire subject of my first grad school course that following summer, Philosophy of Self.

I think I was a bit prophetically ahead of myself in that effort to pull it together after all, despite each new obstacle. The cool part was that I actually learned so much in all its failure. I got to meet some people in the community after attending a meet and greet with the mayor one morning. The mayor took an interest in the vision and met with me and another couple of community members similarly interested in getting some kind of service learning opportunities for high school youth rolling in some program or other. Such a nice man. He really inspired my understanding of a public servant, hosting us past his dinner time in his own home, genuinely concerned for the kids he was serving.

By the time I submit my final report of the class's failure, I had a summary of all it's necessities in this sort of best practices assessment to offer the district after all. So it wasn't a complete loss on the whole. Nevertheless, I felt bad for all their faith in my idea coming to nought. I was warned at the time by my angels that heaven smiles on failed efforts when your heart is in the right place. This was my sort-of consolation.

I had made a difficult decision that spring to leave the classroom after all and pursue studies at University of North Texas, where I'd earned the other masters degrees before teaching. I was accepted into another masters program in Interdisciplinary Studies, aiming to marry three areas of study together in the effort to lay a foundation for a future PhD in something Religion related.

The summer before this last year teaching, I sat cleaning out my garage of former academia files and had this overwhelming sense I'd be going back someday. This was a surprise to me since the last round of education left my head spinning with all that critical theory I loved but was just a bit dense in its intellectuality. I enjoyed the practical realities of "being in the working warrior's trenches" juggling the endless joys and trials of a given day in the art classroom.

For once in my life, I had imagined I would hardly grow tired of this work for at least the next ten years since all my former jobs lasted but a couple years before transitioning into some new chapter. On top of that summer intuition, I had this strange experience stepping into my classroom for inservice after having been home for all the summer. Coming back to the classroom after the summer is a momentous day anyway. But this time, I was overwhelmed with this distinct sense: *this is my last year here.*

I had no plan then, but sure enough, after a season of grappling the realities of leaving my work and wage for another round of study to earn yet a third masters at that, I made the decision to just go for it. I trusted my heart despite all the doubts and prudence of taking classes one by one at night and so on. I composed an entrance proposal and was accepted by May for the summer term. I submit my resignation and embraced yet another new chapter with hope and zeal. My family was hardly at ease in my new choice, but supported me as they always had in each new risky turn of my live-by-your-heart life. Passenger seat views are always more scary than my excitement eating up any sense of anxiety.

So, off I went! Sad to leave behind this family I'd enjoyed for so many years at Marcus High School, but ready to devote my life in it's newest layer to my faith in the pursuit of knowledge about religion and how I could use my understanding to effect my culture and country for good. It was the least I could aim to achieve given my God's generosity to me so late in life. If He would so kindly wake me up to the knowledge of God, then I most certainly wanted to take this new view to it's greatest potential to impact my world the best I could accomplish.

Into the Unknown

S UMMER BROUGHT WITH it the immediate effort to empty my house of all it's furniture in time for the movers the next week. I was relocating to a one-bedroom apartment near UNT's campus and just never got around to such matters as selling furniture piece by piece. Wouldn't you know it, my dear friend of years calls me up one afternoon asking if I'd mind hosting her and her new husband-to-be for a few days the following week.

Absolutely! What a delightful surprise. I was blessed to get to see this girl once, maybe twice a year by this season of our two decades of friendship. She was in love with this new man I'd never met, and I was happy for them. I share this story because it shows how God works and the wonderful things he pulls together as only He can.

I had this one desire for the years I spent furnishing this four bedroom family home in the suburbs: I imagined some magical coincidence of heaven might arrange for a sweet young family that wanted the house as is, furniture and all. That way all my investment and design would serve a more appropriate purpose than a single woman in a family home she figured she could try to fill with a husband and children one day that never came.

While it didn't go quite like the unlikely vision I'd had in mind, I did find my friend looking awfully snug curled into my living room couch taking a nap one afternoon of their visit. Her new husband and I were having a lovely conversation. He was winning me over with his kind, genuine warmth and presence. As I saw her, I made a comment about how cozy she looked, and he agreed.

When she woke up, I offered her the couch as a possible wedding gift if she liked it. She said, "Wow, I've had this intuition we would get a couch as a gift from a friend at our wedding." Done! There went one piece of furniture. As for the rest, it was only natural. They loved all of it and wouldn't you know, they just bought a house that sat empty in need of a full outfitting of furniture for the backyard wedding they had planned just a month or so later.

Furthermore, they had a dream of starting a farm one day, and I had risked quite a bit of dime on this really sweet wooden farm-house family dining table that would supposedly host Bible study art classes that never happened. It just sat there goading me for having bought it for just me after all. I imagined a mom and dad farmer on either end and kids on its benches.

The farmers were my friends! He had three girls from his first marriage under age 13, and she had 2 girls from her first marriage under age 8— almost a Brady bunch I was blessed to witness unfolding in my friend's life. How delightfully it all came together, and just in time to move it all to their home and me into mine the next week. God. A bit different than my vision and yet, such a perfect fit.

I started school in a summer class called Philosophy of Self. While I was immersed in the subject of whether human beings actually have a soul, and if so, what is a soul, and so on, I got to know the Torah finally. Being half-Jewish, this was a relief. I was 36 and just getting around to learning my roots. I recall really savoring the journey through Genesis caravanning with Jacob and his wives.

I enjoyed reading this Law everyone spoke of in Christian sermons about legalism and the new covenant of grace covering the rule book in Leviticus. It was a really fascinating code of ethics to me. It actually made a sort of strange sense, brutal as it may have been then. Gathering fruit after the fifth year of a tree's life—how interesting. Every seven years, an indentured servant earns freedom by the law, and every 50 years calls for a jubilee. All property is returned to its original owner and debts are cancelled. All this made me consider all the talk of national debt. How odd that the law should just erase it as a matter of its practice every so often, rather than let it snowball into some international tripwire of geopolitical interdependence. But, of course! The luxury of ancient times, perhaps, but interesting nonetheless.

I was grateful and amazed at how much it felt like home to be immersed in its narrative. My zeal grew progressively for this new path I was forging. By the fall I had ripened into that pressure cooker of a Jesus-lover sitting through class for the better part of the term quietly trying to understand what the proper love towards Him and another soul is in honor to Him and His will.

It wasn't easy for me. One night, our guest speaker, a Vedanta nun, converted from Christianity in her early teens. I'm "change-your-facing" my way through this guest speaker's visit in a small room with about twelve students. I happened to be seated right next to her at the front. My heart and mind screaming inside: *Why?! Why?! Why leave Him?!* Silence. Stay quiet. Reasons surely you can't appreciate in your ignorance, newbie.

Debates in this class would rage beautifully—nuanced discussions about the texts of Asia. It was a grad-level course called Asian Philosophies taught by this most delightfully enthusiastic Indian professor. Speaker after speaker, topic after topic, I sat quietly considering the nuance of it all. Loyalty. How do you have the integrity of loyalty due a King when His glory is in such a great part about the mercy and wisdom that saves souls?

Somewhere towards the end of my attending classes later in the term, I found myself at home one night in a sudden fit of spontaneous rage— *done! Done with it!!! No more!* There was Tasmanian-me shredding this Buddhism paperback to it's teeniest pieces of paper fiber at home one night. Sick of it. So much detail. So much glorying in distraction and intellect. So much intensity and beauty and gravity to this reality I was coming to appreciate more and more each day in the scriptures and in Christ. And, all against any issue I'd ever cared about as a socially conscientious "activist" bent sort of person. Pressure cooker in me.

Finally, one night there was an article being discussed about America's false title as a Christian nation—in reality, it's more and more Hindu. Fact is good and well. If America, in all her freedom and defense of this unique right to pursue and devote her being as she sees fit, chooses to become more Hindu or what have you, so be it—it was her choice. But, this whole matter had an attitude running through it that just set off the last of my patience. I couldn't stomach the dishonor, bravado, gloating, misrepresentation and so on.

After months of meek participation at best, I sat at home writing a giantly lengthy post for the student discussion board just before heading out to our weekly night class. Sure enough, this night, the professor had the student responses up on the projector for class review, and I sat in utter heart-paralyzed fear, realizing—*Here it is, you must now own your manifesto before these your peers you've quietly seethed your patience all these weeks.*

My turn came up, and it was *soooooo* long. That answer on the screen impressed my eyes to see it there. My words to the class were short. He's not one I'd write off too quickly—this was the gist of it. Inside of little, big me: *RESPECT MY LORD!!!* Is all it came to really. This was spoken in my effort to honor in reserve, at least with my mouth and not typed, vented gospel barfed out. I didn't even remember when it was I actually learned this "gospel" thing anyway. There it was pouring out in rewrite after rewrite at home. All the same: He died for us—we should be so blessed to know such a measure of "justice" for us to contemplate, much less benefit in a divine reconciliation of the soul.

Then, there was the Judaism class in which I literally started revealing steam out my head mid-presentation at the podium—I could feel it. *Pull it back in! You're leading! Get it together woman!* I was presenting on a thinker that ever made freedom of speech and belief possible for me to enjoy worship on Sundays anyway. I spoke of Spinoza, who's writing sparked my ire each morning. It wasn't lost on me that this rebellious, outcast Jew is credited with the foundation of my intellectual and political freedom to even have ire at his writings from then. My father would warn me: *Control your anger.* It's your job to study, basically, not judge. But, love judges, Dad!

I noticed my Christian sister in this class walked about and presented and did all the work in a bubble of poise and peace that I couldn't have contrasted more in my Heat. Respect. Silence. Containment. Containing my growing zeal for a God who, in one near death experience I encountered, warned a man's brief journey to the other side after having a heart attack midst charity bike ride—"Don't make a big deal out of faith in Me when you go back. Just love like I do—unconditionally."

On top of all this tension, the harmony I was accustomed to following was falling apart. I usually tried to be attentive and responsive to my sense of things as an indication of the Lord's will. It always flows in peace when I'm in step with Him through any given day. It's a bit harder to navigate wider swaths of life like months. A school term, for example, is a chunk. If there's no grace to hold the chunk together, it's problematic. Like, back away and figure out why the next step isn't clear.

I was approaching registration for the spring term and felt all this confusion and chaos about classes and instructors and direction. Considering this Master's was all of a few terms in length, this wasn't a good sign going into the second term. I grappled with it and realized I needed help and counsel about how to step forward in this blind leap-of-faith living I'd embraced. I got the answer to my prayers.

Within a few days, three different people I knew broached the topic with me. "I think God wants me to talk to you about your schooling. Perhaps you should reconsider your path? Have you looked into any Bible schools?" Well, not yet. With the third recommendation bearing the same message, I grappled with my choices and the gravity of changing course.

Withdrawing a month before the end of my classes could leave me with an F on a transcript I'd hoped could lead me into a doctoral program one day. I didn't want to risk this given I'd taken half a $20,000 dollar loan out too, after five years of teaching left me half way through paying off a $20,000 ten year note. It didn't make sense, but it was what I'd asked for in my prayer answered quite explicitly.

I finally put away all my grappling when I heard Him one night as I lay there trying to sleep crunching the sense of all this mentally. I heard this in response to my confusion: *spiritual protection.* To withdraw was for my spiritual protection. Strange. Not what I would have expected at all. But also a major relief. Because I had suffered for quite a bit by then. I was tired and traumatized.

I'd been lost in a haze of torment and nightmares for the better part of the term. I'd have to focus my attention, for example, in the Judaism class, on our professor's profuse knowledge base with it's branching tree of details. Focusing was against this backdrop of horrific visuals terrorizing my mind. Shins being skinned, for example. Who sees this stuff? I never did in all my life prior to the arrival of the darkness after converting.

It would just repeat itself like a tape rewinding and replaying. It aggravated me, but the only choice was to focus on my professor best I could. By night, I'd be subject to dreams that were disturbing and seemed to test my fidelity to my new righteousness. In one, for example, I was standing in this long, snaking line with a bunch of people that were half-dead or sick and depressed, gray.

I couldn't figure out what was going on until I caught glimpse of the destination everyone was waiting to reach—a stage where they were stripped of their shirts and a standard number was being carved in blood on their backs! Terrible! Some satanic figure was orchestrating this whole madness, and I was just going along with it. Unacceptable! I left the line to escape from the front of the warehouse that had no wall, incidentally. Anyone was free to go, technically. I ran hard as I could into this sunny meadow, trying to clear a steep hill to get to the other side.

Sure, it's just a dream. Praise it wasn't real! But, who cares? It still adds to the general sense of trauma that was building in my spirit that term until I was a sobbing heap this one day as I confessed to my friend and some women consoling me that I was flat out exhausted. I just cried and cried endlessly. So worn thin.

So, when I heard the reason the Lord wanted me to withdraw that night—for my protection—I got all the answer I needed. I put in the papers that week and began searching out the next step. I ended up visiting two schools the following week and chose the second to apply and subsequently enroll in for the Spring term by that January.

While I appreciated the challenge of all the gray I faced trying to comprehend various situations at UNT, I was awfully grateful to be in this new place born of His love, even in miracle faith, and devoted to it decades later still yet. This new school was something else. I'd stepped into a dream that had come alive 30 years ago with the eyes of faith one couple had in looking on it's former plot of land.

Nothing but an abandoned, unkempt club district with but a building standing in the midst of downtown Dallas remained. Yet, this Spirit-filled couple, Gordon and Freda Lindsay, didn't see trash—they saw God's dream. They bought it and founded Christ for the Nations Institute in the late sixties. It has since blossomed into a full ministry college offering certificates and several Bachelor's degrees in the various areas of knowledge that equip servants of Christ.

Nothing complicated here when I came for a one day, I'm sold done-and-done campus visit a week after I submit my UNT withdrawal form officially. I was like a kid in a candy store—that place felt unreal. So amazing. My friend Sarah Ann said with tickled zeal, "Look, Pedrameh! It's a flag of Iran!" We were walking by an administrative office that had an Iranian flag up in its window.

This was surely the "island of Christians" I sensed in my desperation just before enrolling. Even coming into the first day of orientation, I found myself slammed in the early dark morning. My friend Sarah Ann stopped by McDonald's for a quick bite. As I stepped out of the car, I was sucker punched in my soul with the thought-reality that I was created for destruction. I would either end in hell or cease to be when it was said and done as some sort of prophetically heinous fate.

It's fine enough to just fathom such a belief system for example, but to be personally hit with a truth, well, I just held to the side of the car trying to catch up to her in my dizziness. I figured, *just more spiritual attack—gotta move on, it'll pass.* And it did. I embraced the orientation by morning, doing my best to concentrate. I was quite amazed by this school's presentations and staff. Clearly, this was a really special place. And they had accepted me on such short notice as a late entry after some uncertainty about my status. It all worked out after all.

Sarah Ann made it possible. She said the Lord had told her that I was her "assignment." She helped me so faithfully that fall in so many aspects of my life. Even that morning I wouldn't have known I'd end up there, but that she urged me, "Hurry up! It's time to go!" as we sat at the same Starbucks where I'd met her for the first time.

The day we met some months prior, her Star-of-David necklace caught my eye, and we got to talking. I was interested, given my hopes for the salvation of my father. So I got to know her, and she became my mentor. She had this spiritual insight about life, having walked with the Lord for over forty years. For all the struggles I'd been facing, God sure blessed me with an advocate and help.

Needless to say, that promised spiritual protection was something I searched for hopefully as I entered into this new life in Oakcliff, Dallas. I was grateful and privileged to join the campus, blessed to be accepted. I even got assigned to a single unit in the John dormitory on campus. I found myself setting up my little museum postcard featuring Jesus and the Samaritan woman at the well, from John 4:9.

I loved this verse and this artwork because I always felt like that woman. She had many husbands before Jesus declared to her at that well that she was indeed headed home to the fifth one she hadn't actually married. That got her attention. She believed in Him. Because she honored Him in faith, He spent the next few days ministering in her town. My past bore a similar resemblance to this woman. So, I felt grateful not be judged on this account—to be received instead, just like her. I was also quite tickled to make the connection to my dorm address, apartment 409!

Salvation and CFNI

I SET OUT FOR class early that first morning. The crisp January air cut across my face. Briskly striding with notebook in hand, I suddenly felt reminiscent of a younger time in my life. It was a golden year, if you will. This former time was an age of sufficiency and success in the convictions of my conscience. I was but fourteen, facing the whole of my life's dreams and ambitions with a confidence yet tested against my weaknesses.

I hadn't felt this sense of being for so long. Now, confronted with the absolute privilege and heady reality of actually being a student in this miracle institute, I felt a deep decision take shape in me. I looked out at the sun rising gently on the horizon with a fierce sense of determination marking the moment. *I will make the most of this time. I will give it my all. I will succeed.*

With this sensibility I took to the cafeteria each morning and assembled a plate of health aiming at disciplined excellence. Over the first week, I came to sit across from this one woman habitually, my new friend who seemed to breakfast at the same time as me. I noticed we had different airs about us. She seemed calm and at ease, enjoying her egg and sausage breakfast. I, on the other hand, felt ambitiously rushed and dissatisfied— trying to embrace my yogurt and whatever else seemed a good idea in that frame of mind.

I sensed the Lord pointing out our difference to me and favoring this girl, saying—*See, that is how a child of Mine rests in My generosity and honors Me. You, self-driven and determined one, make Me look cheap, and you seem to think you're boss, on top of it all.* These are, of course, my words, capturing but a sense of comparison that no one is supposed to attribute to the correction and shaping of the Lord. Writing from my current vantage has left me a bit wounded of the shortcomings I face in such a calling and process; hence, the attitude with regard to such a deep matter of saints and centuries as sanctification. Just the slow, devoted, careful shaping of the human into the divine.

It's absolutely tremendous to fathom undertaking such a calling anyway. Abiding in the righteousness of original conscience in all the complexities of attaining to the place you would occupy in your personal purpose in the world—that's huge as it may be for the average soul. Now, set your sights on the role model of all time—mankind's Savior. Then, take a hand at it.

For all it's seeming intimidation, He said to His disciples of the great miracles He demonstrated, *You will do greater things than these.* As a father who intends to see His children shine an even greater light than the one He once bore, He warned them that His children would manifest His presence in time.

When the Lord announced His identity and ministry, He read from Isaiah 61: *The spirit of the Lord God is upon me, because the Lord has anointed me; he has sent me to bring good news to the oppressed, to bind up the broken hearted, to proclaim liberty to the captives, and release to the prisoners...They will be called oaks of righteousness, the planting of the Lord, to display his glory. Isaiah 61:1-3* This school aimed to shape such souls, His present day "oaks of righteousness," into His purpose for their lives.

Each day, class was held in the same large auditorium across the street from the cafeteria. Students were required to swipe their ID's to acknowledge a prompt arrival to morning worship. This was absolutely amazing. What is normally a Sunday morning devotion to glorify the Lord was actually the start of each day. One hour of songs and students raising arms to the King in love of the One worthy, testifying of His greatness. I was possessed, in all my ignorance of salvation then, with the grand magnitude of this reality. This is REALITY. For all the justice man strives to enact the best we know, to fathom it's framed in the gravity of a cross is tremendous.

Then, I still hated that cross, for love of the King. I didn't quite grasp it, like I don't even now. But, I was gripped with this reality: the one word—SALVATION. Salvation was won for mankind by a man barely acknowledged or honored in my culture—at least by me in any life I ever knew before the age of 33. To me, in all my ignorance, he was but another of many religious options in the diversity of the modern day.

My ignorance surely, but I recall angels warning me when I would marvel to another person of my irreverent naïveté after first coming into grace—*Don't put yourself down, there are many like you*—and, apparently, the Lord wants no self consciousness or self-deprecation to stand before the mercy He purchased for souls like me.

After the hour of worship, class began in the same auditorium. Students settled seating patterns the first week of class. I always sat in the front near the stage in the rows of theater seats. I was situated near these sweet girls that were strangely receptive to me. As tormented and demonized as I felt, I didn't always feel like I fit in. So, I felt grateful for these young women. They were the perfect example of what the Lord calls His children to reflect—the light that sets His people apart for the sake of realizing His presence in the world. A Christian is to be the lampstand of His work in a person. This way, everyone would get to experience His reality and hopefully, awaken to faith.

John 5:15-16 states, *No one after lighting a lamp puts it under the bushel basket, but on the lampstand, and it gives light to all in the house. In the same way, let your light shine before others, so that they may see your good works and give glory to your Father in heaven.* Then, in the epistle and letter to the Hebrews, St. Paul wrote: *Pursue peace with everyone, and the holiness without which no one will see the Lord. See to it that no one fails to obtain the grace of God... Hebrews 12:14-15*

These girls were literally lit up. While I never had a gift of "seeing in the spirit" like some are able to see angels and demons and such, I could actually see the bright bubble of the Lord's light on these women. One was so bright, I could see the fuzzy aura glowing golden white about her each day.

She carried herself in a poised peace, and she was so gentle and kind. She shared the story of her conversion and how she changed, becoming the friend at the bar who was contented to order a hot chocolate instead of a cocktail. In her case, her friends took note and followed suit, inspired to try this new ethic. I was taken aback by her story, saddened to remember my first experiences after converting when I found myself in a setting with friends where I had formerly drank with everyone else. I felt awkward instead of contented. I had no idea how to fit in or bear this new way without seeming like I was somehow holier-than-thou for my sudden change.

It never occurred to me that this girl's story could be "the way." Of course! Oh well. This was among many lessons I learned being exposed suddenly to so many others pursuing the Lord. There was a lot to the world of Christianity that was entirely novel to me early on. Much of the language was completely foreign. I'd hear such terms as "the flesh" or "the World" and truly wondered for several years what on earth these things meant in the mouths of so many preachers and peers.

Considering I wasn't free this far into my salvation walk, a few years by this point, I began to search simple scriptures about these terms in my spare time at my desk in the dorm room. *The flesh and the World.* Sure enough, these are key concepts to one's success and freedom standing in the righteousness that is one's calling. The flesh references the "passions" of physical desire—from appetites to anger, insobriety of all manners and self-centered, self-vindicating choices in relationships.

The World was referencing the pursuit of self in life's ambitions—the shallower efforts to compete or succeed at another's expense for the sake of personal glory or greed in material, temporary gains. Set apart from all this is the truth and way of the Spirit—the eternal priorities that would reflect heaven's values on earth. Unfortunately, even though I studied hours worth of lectures recorded by a renowned deliverance minister who actually taught at this school, I never quite managed to apply this knowledge.

It was clear I was very troubled. This minister, Dr. Carol Thompson, had identified dark roots in the soul that open up doors to the Enemy throughout life. Like many deliverance ministers anointed and experienced in the realities of the demonic, he noted that all manners of various life traumas and trials can create the vulnerabilities that plague a person down the line.

One may seek a psychotherapist for childhood abuse, another a psychiatrist for chronic depression; but, in the end, the trauma of abuse at an early age or a deficient coping mechanism in an individual confronted by rejection or divorce, for example, can lead to a broken sense of self and identity or a fragmented psyche that leaves a person exploited by the will of the Devil literally out to destroy and kill them—to rob their life and it's purpose from the earth.

And, in all reality, this exists by my own witness. While it may be a subject of debate, existentially speaking, I would easily consider that the one who dismisses it has enjoyed the luxury of belief by choice. Others desperately pursue help in any fashion it may come, even perhaps willing to surrender to pharmaceuticals yet tested. They are prepared to open up the most personal matters to strangers for counsel.

For at least some of these souls, perhaps troubled enough, the deliverance minister that managed to set a friend free may just be the next effort to find freedom for themselves. Belief isn't always a function of reflection and contemplation philosophically, a matter of intellectual exercise. Sometimes it's a matter of life and death, or at least destruction and misery.

Suddenly, these mysteries became clear to me after so long. I had not put the flesh to death. I was struggling to reconcile the security of my salvation as well as getting free of the demonic. It was helpful to finally understand; yet, shameful that I'd just begun to take note then. Ah, the ever unfolding shame of one's learning curve in the "journey," hoping for mercy to buffer the way of course! A constant discovery of the later obvious. Growing nonetheless!

In fact, the journey to sanctify oneself in the way of the Spirit of the Lord is an awful lot like becoming a reasonable and well-founded adult. Minus all the saintly vestments and the whole issue of holy and it's stature as a concept, the whole "process" really comes down to the common effort to just be the best person you can try to be all the time. Furthermore, the complexity of this miracle of compiled history and inspired pens called the Holy Bible can also be seen simply as a clarion call to salvation in pursuit of the "ancient way," the way of an upright heart.

The Lord encourages the traveler to stand at the crossroads of life and ask and seek the ancient way, the good way, and to take it and find rest for one's soul (Jeremiah 6:16). This, the path of life, the way of heaven—the Kingdom of God—guides one to ever prize the maturity of the Spirit within over the needs of the earlier child mastering the physical and the social, shedding layers of immaturity as he evolves over time.

In this wisdom of living, one steps past the pitfalls that ensnare the "fools," ever mastering one's true purpose and destiny as a person of conscience and righteousness, as someone guided by personal integrity. Back then at CFNI, class left me confounded of deeper matters as my mind grappled with what seemed to be doctrinal impossibilities—things like predestination and free will or salvation by election and so on.

I tried to reconcile these difficult matters, hoping to find help in asking the professor after class only to hear that even he didn't have answers. Hardly unique to any theology effort, sure, but at the time, four hours a day of such curriculum left my head swimming. It was intense! The Dean's assistant later likened such study to water coming through a fire hose on high, particularly given the deep and personal relevance of such knowledge.

In a more accessible assignment in systematic theology class, we were required to write an essay about God's greatest character trait. Truly, not daunting, just exciting! We only had seven options I think. I knew right away what my choice was—not love, not goodness, amongst others, but mercy. It was by the Lord's mercy I ever even came to know of Him. The entire essay came in one easy realization that I would never know any other trait to consider but for the help extended me in early thirties as an adult who needed a Savior and had no concept of such a thing, much less had she fathomed such a reality. Now, I am astounded I ever made it that long without considering the term "savior."

You know who knew this intimate detail about me of course. My Savior. Who covered that human being's entire life in mercy to even make it so far with so little awareness of such a need? The Lord. Now, there's a babushka doll's worth of nested need for mercy stacked against the next—I need mercy for the mercy that once had mercy on my former mercies.

Ultimately, I've had all manners of professional concern about mercy and salvation for the voiceless. I just never termed it as such. In my teaching, I wanted to add to a democratic and critical consciousness that would undo hegemonic forces from within the institution through education and activism. Salvation. Just not a Person everyone needs no matter any construct framing what injustice or which oppressor against which oppressed. The oppressed are any in need of freedom by knowing the truth of life under the throne of a holy judge. Simple, but not obvious without faith.

Especially if the Truth literally traded Himself in for the tragically and cruelly blood-bought purchase of His child just to be his or her personal guide on the way to His home in heaven and eternity. He literally prepared such as heaven and paved it's way painfully for those faithful to His love and sacrifice.

While this gift is offered so generously to a believer in His name, I believe living a life of love and conscience, of honor towards His Spirit, is seen by the Maker whether or not the seen realize they are known or loved. As it is written in 1 Corinthians 13, the epistle chapter about Love, there is a time when we will know fully even as we are fully known. Life is partial and limited for the sake of all manners of purposes that are not intended to arbitrarily deprive a person or divide supposed enemies. Bottomline, the point is to love with all your life.

SHIPWRECKED

Your Name Is Taken From the Book of Life

S O, THE GOSPEL is certainly good news considering sin and justice was covered by a God of sacrificial Love. The ultimate parent, Perfect, happens to be the truth of heaven's rule over the Earth. Unfortunately, it's also heavy news for man to consider the sheer weight of sin and holy justice.

To fathom there is a Judgment weighed against the suffering of the Lord that could rule a person out of the Book of Eternal Life and union with one's Maker is scary as hell, as literally as any testimony of a soul's visit and return could be imagined from the mercy-laden living room I've been writing in.

All that said, I awoke this one morning during my first term at CFNI being informed in my heart by the Lord I ever knew and trusted that my name was being taken from the Book of Life, but my life wouldn't be taken for some time until I learned some lessons. Well, that's about the worst news to discover first thing in the morning, other than losing a loved one perhaps or war impending or some other reality I've yet to know.

I rolled over—my bed was a simple mattress on the floor—and grabbed my spiral journal and pen. Opening it to the day, I jotted the date in the upper left corner. Easy to remember such an anniversary. I documented the night and event of awakening. The words I awoke to were a poison to drink down helplessly. They followed a bad night, too.

It was a Saturday morning. The previous night, I stayed home alone reading this school assignment—an autobiography of the school's founder, Freda Lindsay. I was increasingly lonely in that time, and I recall feeling so grateful she wrote this book. It was so personable and down-to-earth that I felt I spent the evening with really wonderful company. On top of that, her life was an utter inspiration born of a miraculous faith and love for the Lord. So, I was uplifted in my trials and hopes.

Given I had little to eat at dinner earlier in the evening and remembered I had some left over rice in the fridge, I got up to heat a little of it, considering that I ought to just wait until breakfast. I overruled that thought with the consideration that this was an exception, a Friday night treat born of a rare joy to be celebrated without being too much of a stickler. In retrospect, my decision rationalized the tug of the Holy Spirit out of my conscience entirely. Unbeknownst to me, I was apparently in the habit of dismissing these tugs and thus, slowly testing the Lord's patience to the ends of His willingness to wait on my obedience.

After this decision, I battled "religious spirits" that began to chatter in unison about my sin—I insisted, my God is not like that. My God is the God who taught me personally that He defends moderation in such a matter and does not charge a steep judgment against the occasional joy that doesn't stand in the way of a normal discipline. I was accustomed to defending my God in this constant spiritual warfare mentally. I heated up the rice and sat down with my plate and the spirits kept up the mocking chatter.

I ended up goaded into overeating rice. I was really full and sick to my stomach. I felt regret of course. I went over to my mattress and lay down on my belly. I can remember feeling this blanket of absolute dread roll over my body and put me out to sleep. My last thought as I passed out was: *Oh no, I ate too much...*

I had horrible dreams. What I recall was seeing Jesus visit my body and put all my sins back into me. He had cleansed me of so much yuck over the years since my salvation. It was as though He was putting them back. It *felt* terrible, physically. When I awoke and heard the declaration, I was also informed that He was turning His face from me. He let me see it as a visual—His face and light turned away from me.

Given the dread and the dream and the definitive sense of the declaration, I decided I ought to fast. He seemed pleased in this. I fasted two days and realized I had acquired a new demon, a really terrible one. I call it the "demon of blasphemy." It was a spirit that hovered in front of my chest, connecting somehow to my heart chakra. It blasphemed all the time and especially the things of the Lord. So, anytime I saw a cross or heard praise music or tried to take communion and so on, it would speak blasphemy over it so that my neurons got defiled with the association emotionally. I was repulsed by this presence in my love for God. I couldn't enjoy the things of God anymore without getting angry and offended and being mentally ruined.

If I thought of hearts or pink or any of the beautiful kindness, softness, and love God wove into my formerly hardened self and soul, it would all get coupled with defiling blasphemy and hatred so that the love and joy attached to that association got wiped out in my brain and rewritten with filth and hate and depression or despair and such.

I was being reprogrammed literally one word, picture, and thought at a time. I actually witnessed the mechanism and strategy of this "spiritual weapon" that Satan got rights to afflict me with. I was, however, confused—what was my sin? What sin had I commit so grave as to merit such a consequence? Well, given my current struggle with sin and lust and consequence—the sin of gluttony and overeating is no small affair. That's the case for me anyway. I don't think it's some general standard. In my case, it is deeply grievous to God.

I had enjoyed His favor on my life for so long. Since then, I've hit lows of bitterness hearing people striving to receive His "favor." I felt a loathing towards this—like, *He* is the prize, not His favor. You should strive to love and please Him, not vie for His things. Well, that was dumb. Sure, love and please Him, but I didn't appreciate how blessed it is to be worthy of favor in His sight. For Him to look upon you in light—to search your good for His good purposes, overlooking sin and error and prospering your life—that's Favor. How much I desire it now. How much I actually Need it now. Like a miracle of pardon and blessing I need to save me from ruin for goodness sake. All the "favor" people were absolutely right. I was naïve.

I've had a mixed up relationship to an oft quoted scripture that people hold onto for hope's sake through life's trials as a promise God offers to those who love Him. *For surely I know the plans I have for you, says the LORD, plans for your welfare and not for harm, to give you a future with hope. Jeremiah 29:11* Coupled with another promise from the New Testament in the letter Paul wrote the Romans, this creates a true hope for any that love the Lord genuinely. *We know that all things work together for*

good for those who love God, who are called according to His purpose.
Romans 8:28

I felt frustrated to have been a person who loved God with all I had—genuine, intense, pure, and as true as some sheltered, first-world immigrant was able to (knew to) muster in her cross-less existence—and still l lacked sufficient self-sacrifice to match the demands of His justice against me. I loved as much as I felt I had in my ignorant, flaw-ridden, wandering self, and it wasn't sufficient in His sight. I don't blame Him ultimately because I see now how unworthy my effort was in its double-minded, half-hearted reality.

The first commandment states: *Love the Lord your God with all your heart, mind, soul, and strength.* I lacked in strength and perseverance. In the last three years, I ended up backsliding in infidelity and faithlessness, re-embracing alcohol and food as means of coping emotionally and of simply enjoying myself at various turns. I can't argue it. I am not worthy of the blood shed for the forgiveness and covering of my sin. I plead on account of the purity in what love I was able to suffer and muster against righteous condemnation, for the sake of my soul's salvation.

Of course, I am greedy of so much more. For simple goodness sake, I desire the pardon that would grant a simple lot—a chance to be purposed in service and love in a life granted to enjoy the world in the light. In what measure of integrity of conscience I could muster living, I strove to align my life with the wisdom I was able to discern from studying the scriptures. This was for my own good and to invite His spirit back into my heart in what measure He saw fit to renew me. As for Jeremiah 29:11, perhaps I am not worthy—as so many no doubt getting by on the streets or sitting with PhDs in soup kitchens and Salvation Army shelters wouldn't mind a blessed or redeemed lot either. What makes you so special, Pedrameh?

As I would understand myself now, in retrospect, I was not a person like so many: a good person suffering for doing right, holding to a promise of God offered from a prophet of old to keep hope and courage in facing a trial one is blameless of causing. I was instead a relatively sheltered person who had lived the life of a prodigal in many ways and seasons, had enjoyed the fulfillment of this promise more than a handful of times, suffering the bottom for my choices.

If He was gracious to cover me before I knew of Him, applying His salvation to me in the face of my ignorance, then I owed a greater fidelity to the measure of grace granted when I first received His gift. I am now held to the responsibility of honoring that knowledge in my awareness that He is not only my Savior, but in all fairness to all souls, also my Judge.

Discerning the Truth

AFTER BEING WRITTEN out of the Book of Life, I continued on in the same confounding stew of graces and condemnation that most attribute to the battle each believer wages against the powers of darkness. I would pass through a single day, laid flat by justice in one turn, but met with a random intercessor by another turn. One young man who approached me in the cafeteria one day stated that the Lord asked Him to come and speak to me. I explained myself briefly. He advised me to pray before I go to sleep to avoid dreams from the pit and the dark. I tried it that night, and it worked. It worked the next night, too.

But, despite such obvious graces and miracle helps extended to me, I was continually confronted by spirits cursing and demanding I discern what's true. In the process of trying to discern my stand before the Lord, I would be confronted with a statement like, "What's the truth?" At some point I was warned that the true Lord would disapprove of the Bible. The sense of this statement seemed to be that His mercy was more unconditional than the scriptures allowed, that the scriptures misrepresented Him as a violent God that He truly was not.

I considered it. It was tempting to believe this. This was how I felt when I first knew His love in salvation at the very beginning. My instinct wanted to reject Christians I would meet claiming children are born with evil intrinsic to their nature. They would claim everyone deserves hell just for the sin in their humanity, but for the cross and salvation. I questioned these things. Somehow, *my* Jesus seemed grieved at these statements and encounters. I was confused. Looking back, I wonder if perhaps He was grieved of my innocence, though I could be wrong I suppose. There is a Christ on a throne that I believe in now and never considered when He was but an intimate love in my heart.

I always believed and defended the opposite about children and innate evil. I still believe this against the doctrine of "total depravity." Then again, I don't know that doctrine truly. If it's saying we're totally evil without God's spirit abiding in some measure, I believe that. The Bible testifies pretty bluntly. Talk about fear of the Lord. If He takes His Spirit away, we'd end up totally depraved. He warned we'd fight over eating our own children. That's an explicit reality I wouldn't want to mess with. In the New Testament, St. Paul warned that He turns us over to a "reprobate mind," stripping sanctity and sensitivity of conscience, hardening the heart. I've experienced that reality in a measure and to a tee. I know it to be true and accurate.

Nevertheless, the way I saw it, children reflect the innocence of the divine, made in the image of the Creator. In that innocence, by the grace of God, is also a process of maturing the natural ignorance, limits, and demands of their humanity. Maturing exposes every soul to the potential to choose evil either wittingly or unwittingly at various measures of culpability. I think of evil as a potential in all souls insofar as we are imperfect creations being ever perfected in divine love. Though the world may be fallen, I see a God who seems prepared and able to take each soul through a tailored journey of development.

Jeremiah 17: 9-10 states, *The heart is devious above all else; it is perverse—who can understand it? I the LORD test the mind and search the heart, to give to all according to their ways, according to the fruit of their doings.* I always believed the heart's perversity was on account of the tendency to rationalize justifications to indulge impulses or desires latent or known to be wrong—not a given, intrinsic evil in man, although that is also possible, I suppose. Man was made in God's image and called to holiness well before the standard and bar on his soul was raised even higher than the Old Testament law to a stricter level of stringency in the example of Christ.

Christ taught the law that commanded obedience in performance and action was to be embodied in an inward integrity, in a conscience of the heart. He provided His spirit to those who believed on Him in faith, to those seeking such a discipleship to abide in His "law" of the heart. Despite this help, the God of the Old Testament commanded His people to "be holy as

I am holy." The same call applies to believers in the New Testament. The calling never changed. The form of the law and the distributions of grace by faith changed as the grace of guidance by the Holy Spirit was purchased and generously granted by His sacrifice. But, the end has always been to reflect His holiness. What does this look like?

Having just read of persecuted Christians beaten by angry Hindu radicals across the world, I was prompted to consider how they represent Christ to the world. Well, they live the cross in the present day for their enemies to consider the reality of the Savior by their example—this is true Love, this is what it looks like. To lay beaten in a hospital bed for no crime but to worship the One who died for your well being and soul, praying your enemy should know such a blessing, too. No blessing ever earned, but received in the generosity of the same God who loves the ones who beat you—just as He conquered the authority to forgive the ones who mocked and crucified Him. It's astounding and beautiful as a concept. Absolutely Brutal in reality. So, True love is Brutal.

As I searched my salvation at CFNI (and for the years following), I discovered many Christians take salvation to be secure by belief and commitment alone. The rest of one's life is dedicated to producing true fruit to receive commendation from the Lord when faced with the judgment of one's works, a different judgment than that of one's soul. While this is confirmed Biblically and represents the ideal outcome of faith in the Savior, unfortunately the Bible testifies not all will end up this way and it's no guarantee in the testing that will confront everyone.

Nevertheless, given such assurances and understanding in seeking counsel from more seasoned Christians, my question was, how am I so insecure? Why does my Lord show me my salvation is in danger and questionable? So, I took to the scriptures and discovered a key term: "in." To get the graces promised believers of the Lord in the New Testament, you have to be "*in* Christ." This means that you walk in a manner that is worthy of His grace, worthy of the blood shed for your sins to be covered in love and not exposed to the shame and justice they actually merit in the world or afterlife. He said in John 15:

You have already been cleansed by the word that I have spoken to you. Abide in me as I abide in you. Just as the branch cannot bear fruit by itself unless it abides in the vine, neither can you unless you abide in me...My Father is glorified by this, that you bear much fruit and become my disciples. As the Father has loved me, so I have loved you; abide in my love. If you keep my commandments, you will abide in my love, just as I have kept my Father's commandments and abide in His love. John 15:3-10.

The Lord promises to send believers a Comforter and Advocate to teach and lead them into all truth. He expects but obedience and submission in trust to His leading, as a child submits to a Father whose wisdom is without question, whose love is proven beyond measure. Given these helps and expectations, He isn't expecting a believer to suddenly master perfect wisdom with regard to Biblical or holy righteousness. He just wants you to honor and trust His leading you in the Spirit. Literally, if He says, go left, obey. That's sufficient to stay "in the light," alongside simple priorities you can stay conscious of in other decisions you may face.

Love being the point, mercy was the Lord's declaration with regard to justice. To demonstrate mercy is to show kindness towards another's sins and transgressions whether suffered by you or not. It is to help guide or hold to a right account those misled or in danger of suffering sin's consequences if you know the better and have enough rights to teach, guide, and correct in your own standing with regard to the sin.

If there's ground under your feet, and no log in your eye, then it's your very duty to help another out and spare them if need be of sins damaging reality, unless of course, the Spirit calls you in a different direction since His lead is paramount. This is where I failed in the beginning of this story. I denied His lead. It wasn't an issue of morality but of disobedience, no matter the innocence of my intent.

Am I Truly a Job?

T HE TROUBLE I ran into with regard to this call to obey was about trust. There were times when I felt lost following the Spirit's lead. Everything seemed to fall into place uncannily. At the time, I would think: *Surely, this is only accomplished in the miracle of God's knowledge of reality. How could I ever assemble this feat if but for His ability?* Yet, it was not a true fruit. It occupied me, perhaps taught me a lesson, but it wasn't a genuinely productive purpose, at least not in *my* hopes for "produce." It was more in service to justice and education than a bearing of true fruit. I ended up but chasing a conceit.

Proverbs 20:24 states, *All our steps are ordered by the LORD; how then can we understand our own ways?* And, Proverbs 19:21 states, *The human mind may devise many plans, but it is the purpose of the LORD that will be established.* So, in this sowing and reaping, I came to feel a natural distrust of the Spirit, whose priorities in leading me weren't always the ones I would desire or choose for myself, even in my efforts to please the King according to His commandments or calls to righteousness. He wants to either test me or teach me and work out justice; and sometimes, that can take years.

The easiest example of this in the Bible would be the wilderness the Israelites journeyed through in the effort to obey the call to Canaan. What could have been a much shorter trek took forty difficult years. Strange, but to consider the possibility it takes time to train warriors out of slaves prepared to overtake giants. Then, it's rather sensible.

But, along the way, they were called to obey in all kinds of bizarre trust placed in commands that made no sense. Collect flakes that drop from the sky to eat bread, but only take enough for the day. No extra. Why? It will rot. Now that I've met people who have lived by the Spirit for decades, depending on rent from month to month, I see this trains a life of obedience and faith.

Knowing God will provide against the fear of being without, obeying in this trust despite the command's seeming lack of reason, simply to honor God's intent and purposes beyond and irrelevant to your questioning— this is living by faith. I've always admired this trait in others. It is utterly humbling, that measure of trust and honor towards the Lord. I've never surrendered to that extent.

When it was said and done, I began to understand the comparison of my faith walk to Job in the prophesy I had received so much earlier on. In the first year of my salvation, shortly after receiving my calling, I was warned that I was to be tested as Job was in the Bible. Now, seven years later, I see why this warning got issued. Essentially, despite the gift of grace that salvation was to me, the Lord ever intended to take me through a justice journey to both teach me about the sins of my life and to complete some measure of justice in that regard.

To sin against grace is one thing. But to be taken through a journey that metes justice for your sins from childhood, teens, twenties, thirties— your whole life—that resembles Job. Over the course of many verses, Job essentially pleaded, "Please don't hold the sins of my youth against me... The Lord has hemmed me in, it is He who holds an account against me." This is how I felt after some time when I started catching wind of my particular faith walk seeking counsel from Christians and the scriptures. I was *supposed* to be a child of God, set free of the world and the just requirements of the law and it's condemnation. But, I wasn't. Some of it was my sin. But even taking that into account, in all my transparency and search, my situation still didn't add up, and that's at least part of the reason why.

In the sense of divine justice, I seemed to be coming up short somehow when the Lord's sacrifice was *supposed* to be all sufficient. This insufficiency led me to search the validity of losing one's salvation. I've had trouble finding any ministry that actually acknowledged a Biblical support for losing one's salvation. Perhaps in contrast to former seasons of church preaching, there is a prevalence of "grace doctrine," it seems, at this time.

I would question this doctrine, frightening as that may seem, for the sake of true security and personal diligence with regard to so deep a matter as one's salvation.

Once I actually found a ministry acknowledging this possibility, I felt relieved to find such thinking if for no other reason than to find someone able to explain my mental torments. At one point, I felt so goaded mentally for being a thief to consume food and resources without earning my keep that I almost chose to give in to the constant commands to kill myself. Resenting God for my undelivered torment, I decided, *Fine then, I'll just settle the matter in suicide, Lord.*

As I stormed off down the street to accomplish this end, angels warned me, *The Lord will send you back and painfully piece you back together so much does He want to fulfill your destiny.* Well, what on earth?! If that's the case, what is this constant condemnation in my brain? And what destiny? I can't even find a job to help pay for my spare bedroom as a thoughtful houseguest and person trying to save money to continue my purpose. So, I turned around and went back to my life. Okay…

Besides, I'm not messing around with Jesus. I've read enough near death experiences. If He's not done with you and it's not your time, He's got the Final Word. I'd rather stay put in one whole live piece and aim for this future He apparently wants. At one point, I was actually "offered" my destiny by the declaration and delivery of angels—*Do you want your destiny?* Well, I mean, of course I do. But, considering a destiny is a blessing so great that I can't ask for it but to be blessed to receive it by the King's sovereign will and judgment, I didn't answer them. I just bowed my head and prayed, *Your will be done, Lord.*

I loved my Lord. I wanted whatever He desired. If He saw fit to bless me with a destiny, I was willing to receive it with gratitude, knowing it was no accomplishment I could ever take credit for when it was said and done. I wouldn't even want to or care but that His purpose in granting it be fulfilled and that I should be so blessed as to partner with the One I loved in serving goodness for His glory. To go Home one day to that end, that's the ultimate blessing.

The Hope of Glory

J UST BEFORE DEPARTING for CFNI, I heard angels warn me, *You have the hope of glory in you.* I didn't understand the statement though I trusted it because it was one of those Christian phrases I'd heard enough times that I knew it was somehow true even if it never quite made sense to me. Now, now I understand. His spirit in my heart shining in love for the world to understand His truth and reality through me—that's the hope of glory, that brings His Father glory for the measure of His sacrifice.

He desired that His adopted children receive the heaven-home He prepared for them. In His love, He desired to share with them all things eternal—material that does not corrupt, to be appreciated with a sensitivity to perceive beauty unfit in the world of life's temporary trials. He desired to share His own glory with an eternal family, prepared to love and honor such a Father in His timeless reality. As the scriptures describe, heaven is the best place to invest one's heart.

In Luke 12:32-34, He explained to His disciples: *"Do not be afraid, little flock, for it is your Father's good pleasure to give you the kingdom. Sell your possessions, and give alms. Make purses for yourselves that do not wear out, an unfailing treasure in heaven, where no thief comes near and moth destroys. For where your treasure is, there your heart is also."*

Christ was said in the scriptures to be the first-born in a family of brothers and sisters, having run the race for the sake of His brethren—to secure their victory and set their example in His loving covering of their falls and imperfections. So, this was the "hope of glory" He died to bring to life in those who would receive His gift in belief and faith that He is their Savior and Lord reigning on the throne of Heaven with His Father over creation.

It sure would have helped me to understand all this then. I was supposed to claim and declare my true identity in the sacrifice my Lord made for me, His child, against the wiles of the Devil. The enemy desired that I should not know or claim my true Identity in the Lord's cross.

The hope of glory is that by the grace of the cross, I could rise into the only identity that truly matters in light of the love expressed by my holy Judge—that of a son or daughter, loved beyond sin and beyond such identities as she acquired in a life of sin and error. This reality matched the God who warned me in the beginning not to be consumed by hell for my sins of old. He showed me that I am loved by my Heavenly Father despite any sin beyond my own recognition of His love or my ability to honor it.

That child was innocent. My ignorance then covered my debt to the Lord who paid my debt. Now, I have understanding and the burden of knowledge and culpability. For all those who insist there is no sin the cross didn't cover, I see a scripture whose intent is to silence any boasting under a Holy Judge.

It is simply not true of divine justice towards sin, at least in my case, sins against the grace of the cross. In the book of Hebrews, the apostle Paul warned: *For if we willfully persist in sin after having received the knowledge of the truth, there no longer remains a sacrifice for sins, but a fearful prospect of judgment, and a fury of fire that will consume the adversaries. Hebrews 10:26-27*

While I wasn't and am not willfully sinning in anyway that I haven't shared in this account or that has denied me a measure of grace ultimately, I have suffered consequences according to a justice I've surely merited. In all fairness, people face the same complex task of accomplishing justice in the world. Fine lines must be discerned to draw a distinction and relativity in the severity of an offense, and thus, determine an appropriate penalty before one's debt to the law or society.

Now, I'm left with the burden of my sin's debt, hoping before my Lord for enough grace to cover a service or purpose in love and not shame for my past, having dishonored graces along the way. Now, I wish I'd "fought the battle" back when I got that warning about the hope of glory as I should have. I imagine I wouldn't have likely ended up resorting to some of the sins I ended up leaning on for support when I was faced with stress and instability.

Now, I recognize this literal presence of the Lord's spirit in my heart because I've *lost* a good deal of it. That presence was the hope of being sanctified to His good purpose that others might know His love and mercy by feeling His presence in and on me. I've felt it diminish progressively, especially over the last couple of years as I was pressed in stress and trial.

In reaction to feeling misunderstood and falsely accused in the face of what I felt was my love and good intent, I ended up correcting and "schooling" others in how to respect me and God. These were the very souls, blind in their reactions to me that needed His love and mercy, not self-righteous rebuke.

In one example, I really disappointed the Lord in my behavior and reaction. I had an opportunity to reflect love and instead responded indignantly in my pride. I felt hurt striving to explain my misunderstood self and grew tired of feeling neglected a simple benefit of the doubt by friends or family who simply couldn't relate to me. This particular girl was someone I admired.

She confronted me on Facebook, confused and distraught of my stand, suspect of me for becoming this different person in my understanding in the Lord. I never stated any stand on abortion. Then I came out and stated I was against the funding of Planned Parenthood. I meant no ill. I was no enemy. And it was up to me to recognize that reality.

If I don't see the battle lines the way she appeared to see them when looking at the one she presumed a friend, then it was up to me to reflect that love and reality to her so the true battle lines could become apparent in the process of working out our understanding across the division of perspectives. I regret that I had such opportunities to reflect the love and mercy of my God and failed each one in the hurt and pride of my weaker humanity.

I've heard of so many reconciliations miraculously forged in the Spirit's ability to weave broken relationships back into wholeness. I know and trust in the Lord beyond any other means of healing a breach. It's just a matter of meriting such a grace in His sight. I don't imagine I am in the standing right now that would bring such a grace upon myself, much as I believe, appreciate, and hope upon it. It is up to me to try to reconcile my own walk first.

Purpose is Paramount

T HIS PAST WEEK, I've awoken to warning after warning in my spirit that I could face the ruin of my reputation in the exposure of the porn I watched the year before I got saved. To fathom this is slightly mortifying. The only reality worse to me, other than maiming or what have you would be to go to hell forever. This was the other warning I got all week: I deserve hell. If I was to die, that's the judgment I'm currently under. I don't doubt it. How do you deal with that?

I commune with my heart in the night; I meditate and search my spirit:

> *"Will the Lord spurn forever, and never again be favorable? Has his steadfast love ceased forever? Are his promises at an end for all time? Has God forgotten to be gracious? Has he in anger shut up his compassion? Psalm 77:6-9*

It's hard to believe a Psalmist could so perfectly express one's condition. I've known a whole lot of grace I never deserved in my life. Now, I'm getting to experience the just end of mercy. Blood covers sin, but if sin offends blood how much worse the cost? So, I'm left in a spiritual justice bind with decisions to make.

For example, should I accept an offer to take all the crazy this has spawned in my behavior to a rehab facility on the east coast like my generous father is offering? If not that, where should I take myself? If I can't hold down a job because I'm too distracted and distraught then where or what should I pursue given the warnings?

I'm realizing in this space mentally: If I don't know when I might die, and a good portion of my struggle with rebellion and sin is frustration over a loss of self and purpose so that I "act out" against my reality by eating and drinking what I shouldn't be, then I need to A. Stop eating and drinking and sinning, and B. Search out a meaningful purpose for what's left of my life ASAP.

These warnings have been with me since the start of September, and it's now approaching the end of October. Does this make any sense? The extent of my rebellion with eating and drinking consists of failing to fast when I feel I'm being manipulated mentally, or when I feel betrayed in the spirit. I was once warned that I had a "constant presence of evil" and a "deeply powerful mocking spirit."

All this was good and well for many years. Terrorized as I was, I had the grace of pressing forward in a battle against an enemy in my love for God and into God's love for me. As I backslid, the "spirit of anti-christ" I acquired at CFNI got more and more powerful. Slowly, I got steamrolled by this presence. It grew harder and harder to hold to love. Now, I fast to get free from evil, but I have a hard time staying faithful in my fasting vows because of the mental cruelty. I end up reaching for comfort.

Nevertheless, this has been the large portion of my sin and disobedience. I put drinking away for the most part. I haven't drunk alcohol in the last year but for a handful of times when I've been faced with extreme desperation. And then, this is strange as any warning or decree about dire justice facing me: the other week the Lord led a woman to confess to me, "The Holy Spirit fell on me in church two weeks ago and asked me to tell you that God loves you and wants you to stop fasting for some time and to let your friends take up shifts fasting for you."

Furthermore, amidst all these declarations, the Lord warned me: *Your hope for salvation rests in a relentless pursuit of your Lot.* What sort of sense is that? How does pursuit of my lot balance justice in any way? It's like, essentially, if I can persuade my Maker that I'm good for fulfilling my highest purpose in a destiny on earth, then He will grant me the chance and the grace I need on my debt. Otherwise, I'm in deep and owe more than I could ever settle, and it seems I've used up the grace His blood bought, so I'm at the end of myself.

Literally, He suffered that cross not just for my soul but for my purpose and service. If I squander my purpose, I've wasted His sacrifice. On this one account did I have hope of redemption and overcoming. It's good to have any hope, so for that I am grateful and strengthened. Nonetheless, I stumble and struggle to muster the courage, faith, and fortitude to prove myself worthy. It's just a bit demoralizing. It seems even *He* sympathized with my trial through the testimony of the woman from church.

All this said, I feel I am left with one paramount concern: *Purpose.* At one point, I remember in my desperation feeling a crazy need to use my gifts in service—like just get yourself to a dean's office for a doctoral program and talk to someone and see what they may offer in the way of defending your development for goodness sake.

Not the typical application procedure. No one wants to accommodate a crazy woman worried she may lose her shot at a life worth preserving in any measure, be it in length, service, or soul. Yet, what else would I do? The urge was immediate—like, put yourself on the line—you have nothing to lose. Be relentless. Strangely, just like the Lord warned me. The basic sense was, if I succeed in making myself useful in a purpose or service, I would somehow dodge all this justice threatening my ruin. I don't get it, but clear as day have I endured all of this spiritually.

So, in this urgency, I felt this pressing: If not one office, then go to another, until someone hears you and decides to take you on. Nothing to lose. OR, go "heal" your woes on a farm with group therapy and recovery teams to help you pursue your dreams. If I actually had any sense I'd receive the offering, it would be quite the grace to heal and determine dreams and such.

I just don't know if that's going to happen. And if not—why so much cost to pass time in a more pleasant place than the streets? Why not pursue purpose instead? Because my mind and "ability" are compromised. It's like some catch-22 of Salvation Sinsanity. I've considered hiking the Appalachian trail. Some kind of nature vs. man feat of overcoming more worthy of calling life and trial than this which I'm enduring.

I've considered homelessness. Since, I *am* technically broke if not for my father's provision. Why not embrace the Truth and live it instead? Well, as with the trail, I'm not experienced in either the real woods or the streets and so, I'd likely beg bears and beatings that would later inconvenience the same family that pays cleanly out of their pockets for now. Dead ends if being thoughtful in one's considerations.

I've tried tailoring it down. Perhaps a shorter camping trip or packing a tent for the streets? Then my angels seem to consider the pain in the behind I'd be to heavenly entities on top of my material family. Great. Hmmm. Oh, it is *sooooo* grievous to fathom the cost of the healing farm. What insanity are you healing exactly in doing this farm?

Well, there may just be no more sane and sobering of an insanity as discerning the legitimate validity of one's security of soul before a Just Judge. To fathom death, well, that's a trying enough subject for the average person of maturity. Mortality wasn't even something I'd given much deep thought to by the time I converted at age 33, for all my philosophical and contemplative tendencies in life.

Dying is a tough enough reality to face honestly. Now, throw in the notion of eternity and the eternal. That's a pretty bizarre reality to fathom, too. All I've ever known is time. To imagine timelessness with no end bends my ability to imagine. I used to be disturbed even by the thought of living forever, in heaven, much less hell.

Why would that be disturbing? No end to goodness and joy, to one's self? That should be undeniably good. But, for some reason, I found it disturbing. It seemed more natural that all things have a span and an end. I can't imagine why that might be. So many believers seem utterly content in resting in a forever of existing. Therefore, I believe it is a province of the Holy Spirit's conviction of the soul. Surely, God places that comfort in the person. It is not born of my "natural," material existence for me anyway.

For the time being, I've decided to submit to my family's desire and lead. I know God works through all means as there is no limit to the instruments at His hand. I've slowly learned to discern hopefully with more accuracy when it is I ought to take His lead through another or others, believer or not. For now, I'm going to trust my family is the instrument of His grace.

Besides, I should be so blessed to be afforded a chance to work through this matter on a healing farm with others grappling with highs and lows, voices, addictions, and existential concerns. Whether the woes are classified or categorized as one or another disease, we're all reconciling our reality against the demands of the world and existing. It's all life as they say and one way or other, we're dealing with being a piece of god in God.

Vision of a Dream

I T'S ONE THING to abide in insights attained by self-examination and personal growth. It's another to actually become true in light of the reality one's steeped in. I realized recently that I'm like the old childhood story I loved as a little girl, "The Velveteen Rabbit." This little stuffed animal wanted more than anything to become Real and be able to play with all the real people and animals instead of waiting for her owner to choose her among her toys. So, the rabbit hoped to receive enough love in time, tattered and worn as she was being a doll, to take up movement one day as a Real animal and friend.

Eventually, she was loved to life. It's a beautiful and brilliant childhood tale. I feel like: *I'm slipping through the cracks of life and existing. I can't seem to keep my soul or days afloat properly.* I know I need to stop sinning, and I know I need to fast to seek reconciliation; and yet, I struggle to do what I know to do in my frustrations and failures. Right about now, I find the trials of the apostle Paul heartening. For starters, he apparently suffered not only a "thorn in the flesh," but also dealt with "cruel messengers" and strong sinful impulses. In the book of Romans, he says of his frustrations:

> *For I know that nothing good dwells within me, that is, in my flesh. I can will what is right, but I cannot do it. For I do not do that good I want, but the evil I do not want is what I do. Now if I do what I do not want, it is no longer I that do it, but sin that dwells within me. So I find it to be a law that when I want to do what is good, evil lies close at*

hand. For I delight in the law of God in my inmost self, but I see in my members another law at war with the law of my mind, making me captive to that law of sin that dwells in my members. Wretched man that I am! Who will rescue me from this body of death? Thanks be to God through Jesus Christ our Lord! Romans 7:18-25

So, at least I'm not alone in the struggle! Nevertheless, I couldn't help but feel perhaps my difficulty was misplaced. Something wasn't right. All this focus on sin and consumption. To consume to cope with the stress of the consequence of consuming? Really? Surely the heart of the matter runs deeper. What's missing? I don't have a center. There's no point. There's no driving desire. There's no purpose. There's no vision. There's no dream. The center of my being has nothing to reach for.

So, without any anchor in the middle or a sight to set my eyes on for goodness sake, for the sake of life and not death, I saw the whirlpool of my circumstance in a different light. Perhaps such an anchor would help me. I started considering particular questions. What if by some unforeseen mercy, I manage to merit heaven, but I would lose days on earth? Then what is my regret? What I neglected to risk and dream and do?

Normally, I would say my greatest regret would be the damage I caused those I could have loved better. If not for the self-centered ambitions that overshadowed my family's efforts to love me, I would have lived a far more noble priority than self-pursuit for so much of my adult life. The irony. Now that I have no ambition but the desire to untangle myself into a productive stability, I lack the focus of an ambition that isn't self-pursuit but rather captures my soul in a dream and greater purpose. One way to honor loved ones is to seek to fulfill all the love that believed in me and invested in the hope of my contribution in the world.

What's especially hard to consider is the hope they cherished when I wasn't looking, when I was too selfish and self-absorbed to notice. So, strangely, this farm declares it's mission to be helping these struggling souls find their dream and pursue it. I stayed up all night yesterday considering purpose. Suddenly, I witnessed all these pieces falling into place.

As it turns out, with the help of the Lord, I *do* know what I would hope to do with a blessed chance at my future. In fact, it seems I know it rather clearly. Now that it's before me, I can also say I desire it firmly and truly.

I feel confident I would do this particular vision justice in the freedom of my mind and in the security of my soul in the blessing of my Lord.

So, here's the short story of my dream: I've always enjoyed and seemed to have a knack for counseling. From childhood, I tended to be the ombudsman-like figure in friend circles. I negotiated and brokered relationships breached in disagreement and confusion. I even counseled my parents at times when they had trouble communicating and misunderstanding seemed to divide them falsely.

My parents often encouraged me in my confused twenties to pursue a career as a family therapist. Of course, at the time, I was too immature to appreciate what a tremendous compliment and expression of faith this was in me. I had no desire to be a counselor then. It felt so laborious and heavy to me at the time. I wanted to have passion and joy in my work.

Teaching high school art was the epitome of my dream job. Since leaving the classroom four years ago, I had originally set out to learn world religions, the Bible, and ethics in contemporary global issues. I wanted to make the most of the impact God's saving grace made on my life and my understanding of reality. I wanted to give back.

Despite all the hardship of these few years, there was what seemed to be a genuine effort to discern and pursue my "destiny," which is a rather grand concept in the face of such a messy spiritual circumstance. Nonetheless, the Spirit did defend and stand by my side in many ways to that end. The Lord often warned me to use my time meaningfully when I couldn't figure a more meaningful avenue open to me.

On one occasion He even warned me not to make light of my destiny because it means a lot to Him. My friend called me one day declaring in some strange sense of anxiety or urgency: *What have you done to change the world?* This stood out to me because it was drenched in my intuition with this odd sense of urgency, like: *You're supposed to do something bigger than this with your life. You're missing your window.*

At the time, about a year and a half ago now, I remained lost in the mystery of my being. What was I supposed to be doing that I couldn't figure out and attend at the time? I literally spent those days looking for work and studying side projects to try to help friends with whatever skills I had acquired in my former education. I also researched professional education options, picked up trash from especially littered strips of town, and listened to endless testimonies and sermons online. I did what I knew to do.

The issue of my changing the world was truly a mystery to me. Who cares anyway? Why should it matter to my friend of all people? To change the world? What on earth. Now, just last night, after all these insane stakes, a dream for my future seemed to just fall into place on a simple page of my journal, right before my eyes.

My Lord (that I seem to be having the hardest time appeasing) apparently sees ways to fit all kinds of things together in one life. He helped me lay out a vision that would realistically marry my desire to counsel, be creative, learn ethics, and serve social justice causes into one path. A Master of Divinity would allow me to develop knowledge of biblical ethics and pastoral counseling. Then a phD in Public Health would allow me serve in foster care like He's led me the last year or so. Now, I realize all that's super ambitious given my current lot, but it is a dream after all. I'll be blessed to finish any step of it, one chunk at a time. With God, all things are possible.

What was interesting is that He showed me that my interest in arts therapies is actually something I could develop during the MDiv through selective attendance of workshops. It was perfect, and nothing I was able to conceive of my own effort. So, I sat there happy-as-could-be staring for the first time at my life's dream, spelled out crystal clear on a single page. How exciting!

I came up to the importance of purpose, recognizing some of my struggle with sin is the lack of center in my life. God provided, reminding me of a proverb: *Without a vision, the people perish.* Like, in the reign of a just king, he is charged with providing people with a wise rule and a vision of their place in the righteous demands and realities of the world and the trials confronting their society. If the king fails to lead in this way, the people are naturally and innocently lost. The burden rests on the king. This was me, lost for lack of vision. So, my King provided.

Relating to Hope

NOW THAT I have vision, I have a responsibility to relate to it properly. I don't really know what I'm doing so far. First, I was overjoyed. Then, I was confronted with the distinct fear that I'm presumptuously confident to even imagine it has any possible hope of becoming real. Then, I missed a million signs of grace coming through my parents and completely trampled their efforts to point me in the right direction with regard to this seeming turn in my fate. I yelled at them yet again in my frustrations at being a failure.

Anger and yelling is about the worst sin, far worse than my consumption issues. Proverbs 20:20 states, *If you curse father or mother, your lamp will go out in utter darkness.* While I didn't curse my parents, yelling is close enough. Especially when they were trying in their own way to encourage their cynical, bitter child to believe again. Weary of believing because it's sin to even hold this dream in my hand in light of my current stand, I took to the streets yelling at the sky, again. I came back home apologizing to each of them, again. What use is a constant apology? Just don't scream in the first place. But, it was too late.

Then, I check my Facebook to discover my mother had sent me a video link that same morning I sat rejoicing at the conceiving of this dream in my journal. It was a short life story of this woman who suffered immense injuries in a car accident. She had to piece her life and purpose together from a completely reframed reality that left her divorced and unable to bear children or walk again. She was informed by doctors that her life dream to create art would be impossible because of her injured hand.

She refused. She refused to be barren. She adopted a son. She refused to be bound. She took her wheelchair to the streets and the TV screen in an abundant life serving her nation. She refused to deny her dream. She demanded art supplies from her hospital bed and began painting her soul's suffering for herself alone. She said she stopped caring of pleasing another, but became satisfied to please herself. It seems she overcame her trial in her determination to be true to her soul and to live fully.

My mom was talking to me, literally nudging my soul in light of my dream page, in light of my desire to take a chance at living something if I have nothing to lose anyway. What really touched me is that the counseling dream I picked up suddenly was about arts therapy in trauma victims and broken families. I'd spent the morning searching institutes that equip counselors to use the arts as a means in their counsel to help people heal.

I felt so bad for yelling at my mom. She is one of the people I've always longed to please with my life and my success in it. Now, she's saying—live true for yourself, but live already. And, I was still bitter and angry towards her because I feel I've failed and I'm tired of being the failure. My apology literally left me standing there, yet again, promising her I'd do my best to succeed at becoming something one day, something that would make her proud.

Anyway, the point is that my parents have both invested a great deal of pride and faith in me. I want so much to make good on their hearts' kindness towards me, especially in the face of my liberality towards grace. This would be my plea to any young person: *Never neglect your Future. You have One Future. Be wise. Take into consideration, and as early as possible, the fact that you are absolutely Unique. There is only one of you in this world. And this one You is divine and gifted for a contribution to life that no one else is able to make in the way that you were designed to create and exemplify.*

There's just one hitch. You are every bit free to compromise yourself, your potential, your gifts, your future at each turn that you neglect your deep worth. It is SO not worth it. Don't sell out. Be expensive, because you are. That's the worth your own Maker and Savior ever saw in you and ascribed to you in His definition of Loving you. He created and covered your life and future, your purpose in this world. Journey with Him. You might just come to know Your Divine Destiny.

I step off my soap box now. Why can't I live by these words myself, right now? I'm not young anymore. But, what difference does it make really? I sell out everyday. Literally, everyday, in my own battle mentally dealing with my mind's landscape of cruelty and shame. I suppose I imagine a young person has a chance to yet avoid all the mess I'm dealing with in facing my hopes and dreams for a future with such uncertainty due to my shaky foundation.

So, how do I assess a true hope? Is this vision granted me founded in genuine faith? It felt like truth and faith, but perhaps in a tentative reality according to daily fidelity, I imagine. Choose rightly day by day, and reach for it—one step at a time. In fact, come to think of it, that's exactly what my mother said when I saw her the other day: *There is always hope Pedrameh, just take one step at a time.*

Christians Aren't Violent

PSALM 11:5 STATES, *The LORD tests the righteous and the wicked, and his soul hates the lover of violence.* Apart from all the violence I just described as a sampling of my behavior recently, the Lord accounted me a fake and a con about a month ago now. Boy did that day hurt. I was shocked. I knew it had to be true, but I was loathe to see how. He showed me I was a wolf in sheep's clothing. Exactly who I'd never ever want to be in a church. Heavens.

I am not entirely sure I understand this fully yet; but, I believe I was a wolf in that I was violent in moments like I just was with my parents, and these events weren't apparent to people who knew me at church. All they see is a seemingly kind and peaceable human being, not someone so frustrated as to curse the sky ranting down a trail in a quiet neighborhood on a sunny day. I was not a Christian in right standing as I appeared or presented myself to be, receiving the grace and love of those walking in purity with the Lord.

I've been called to be meek. To be long-suffering. It's not my job to vindicate wrongs done to me. I am to stay quiet and peaceful allowing vengeance and justice to belong to the Lord, as He is the better judge, not me. This is, of course, challenging. I know my case so well; and, at this point, I'm often quick-tempered in my frustrations to settle it in complaint or insistence on my truth and innocence to whomever. If it's not done in my timing and sense of justice, then my instinct wants to settle it myself.

There is the parable of the unforgiving servant (Matthew 18:23-35) that Jesus told of a man who pleads his debt before a just judge. He is not able to pay it and asks for mercy to overlook his debt. The judge grants it. The man leaves free. When one of his debtors later asks the same mercy of the man, he treats his debtor harshly and denies him freedom, holding him to a stiff account. The judge then calls the man's debt back upon him for his double standard.

This is the equivalent of my self-vindicating behavior. It is simply unacceptable and brings judgment upon myself. I may want to prove my innocence. But, it's not mine to prove. And I'm hardly without guilt. The thing about being a con, though, was frustrating to me, and wounding to my heart's intention in that I meant no ill. I don't mean to lead a double life, though I suppose I am, in a way. I would confess my sins and even take leave of the community if that was appropriate or God called me to do this. I don't mean to lie or hide anything.

Also, there is the issue of sharing one's life in the wisdom of love and righteousness, too. I don't always understand what I'm doing. When I've been in better standing in the Lord, I've known a different understanding of sin, and it involved a sense of privacy and covering that was not founded on secrecy and bad intent or hypocrisy.

The Lord has pointed out to me many times that He doesn't like me to expose even my own shameful experiences in self-deprecation or humor that mocks me. Obviously, this is hardly the same as hypocrisy or secrets. But, I was always a bit surprised of this because I only think to act this way in a sense of humility for the sake of sharing some lesson or point about my own mistakes or something.

No. He values dignity and glory. He wants a sense of privacy to cover His child for the sake of glory. Memories that may be special He would prefer to keep private rather than expose them even if my intention is to share for goodness sake, to bless others. He values the privacy more.

There's also the sense of burdening others with information that may not be appropriate for them to know. So, there's the consideration of another's life and burden towards you. As much as it may feel good to be clean of any personal charge of hypocrisy, there is no excuse for saddling others with personal matters best dealt with "in-house."

Recently, I took my frustrations with my ensnarement online to Facebook. I wanted to be honest. This was especially important because I have a history of zealous evangelism, proclaiming my gratitude for God's grace on me and celebrating and praising His goodness and works. While much of my evangelism has ceased, I still can't resist sharing stories of His grace on the lives of other people, His goodness in all those testimonies I've mentioned.

I also wanted to ask for support. Somehow, I need a grace or intercession I'm unable to manage on my own, much as I also need to carry my own load. I wrote many messages to post. Each one had issues. Too much information, too specific. No one needs to know all that. Surely others have problems too and they never burden the crowd with their personal struggles in all the detail no one needs to be exposed to randomly. Too little information, and I end up cryptic and confusing in my plea. Do I declare, for example, that my "broken relationship" with God involves accusations of being a con and a judgment that damns me?

That's a bit drastic for others to be saddled with, true as it may be. As it stands, just confessing this to individuals produces a reaction and burden I don't want to incite in my sharing. In my search for counsel from those I trust around me, people have consistently rushed to refute my doctrine and understanding. No, you're confusing the voice of God with Satan. Satan condemns, not God. God loves you, and His love is unfailing and faithful even when you're faithless. It's scripture. It's undeniably true.

For me to sit and argue a billion other scriptures that confirm God's judgment just to try to defend my God to someone else is a futile and tiresome waste of other people's love and time. They just want to encourage you. What else would they do? What would I do confronted with such a heavy burden confessed to me? I may not dismiss it so readily just because of my personal experience, but it's still a matter to be disclosed in wisdom.

Apart from the burden being presented another, there is the issue of the future and the hope of reconciliation to a productive purpose, also. For example, my sins may or may not strike some as grievous sins if they realized my gluttony has a range from nibbling a handful of Triscuits in pretty severe anxiety to occasionally overeating at a meal to binging and purging in more desperate occasions. Having spent the better part of my twenties bulimic, the impulse comes back to haunt me sometimes.

Gluttony is an easier subject to describe or discuss than porn. I'm ashamed to say I was teaching high school at the time. My watching porn was so divided in my mindset from my teaching that it never occurred to me how terrible my actions were. The Lord has shown me I pursed "knowledge of casual depravity." These words were His way of assessing my sin.

At the time, I never gave thought to accountability. When I came to realize God was real, I was no longer alone or unaccountable. My double-minded reality came to an end. I somehow perceived myself (and truly was a dual person) a caring, devoted teacher (who watches porn every so often?). I have no idea how I lived that way looking back. It's a really bizarre measure of corrupt hypocrisy that I was ultimately oblivious to even if I knew myself to be a rebel-pothead double-life art teacher. Anyway, I watched only from time to time. I noticed eventually, I never watched again after realizing God is real. I couldn't imagine watching and knowing God's real and watching me. I was way too self-conscious, never mind I didn't want to displease the Lord in love for Him or that my view of life and sex changed radically. Porn objectifies what was meant to be sacred. And private. It's crazy, but I flinch and turn from kissing in movies now. That's not me. That's the Holy Spirit's presence rewiring my sensitivity to sin and righteousness. So I deduce, innocent as even kissing may be, it's still special and private to God.

Hard as this is to believe as I look back on my own depravity, Grace covered ALL my sin when I got saved. I can't imagine how Jesus loves someone so awful so completely, so intensely. But He does—at least He did me. Nevertheless, I'm struggling with the devil's rights to try to ruin me by exposing my sin and past in His justice. Of course, in the event that one either denies or forsakes grace, the Bible also says iniquity will be exposed, and all that is done and said in the dark will come to light and be shouted from rooftops. So, there is this effort to "cover" that which shouldn't be exposed for honor and glory's sake; and, there is also this effort to expose for justice sake.

The epistle 1 Peter 4: 8-11 states, *Above all, maintain constant love for one another, for love **covers** a multitude of sins... Like good stewards of the manifold grace of God, serve one another with whatever gift each of you has received. Whoever speaks must do so as one speaking the very words of God... so that God may be glorified in all things through Jesus Christ. To him belong the glory and the power forever and ever. Amen.*

Love covers sin. It doesn't ignore sin, diminish or dismiss sin, deny sin, or joke of sin, but it does cover it for glory's sake. Like I shared, the Lord has warned me not to share shameful stories even in self-deprecating humor for the sake of teaching or sharing a lesson learned. He was that loving towards my past. Even the innocent stories merited the covering of love. When considering confession for the sake of transparency and integrity, then, there are all these angles to contemplate in the effort to honor God.

Sometimes, I am truly astounded at how long I went through life without even considering the possibility that an anthropomorphic Father God exists as Judge. I was atheist or agnostic, and I gave thought to morals and ideals, but boy was it unwittingly pocked with hypocrisy and presumptive prejudice. It was hard enough getting it right without God in all my subjective humanity with it's layers of unconscious conditioning and coping socially.

With regard to those committing evil against the innocent, Psalm 10:12-14 pleads on their behalf: *Rise up, O LORD; O God, lift up your hand; do not forget the oppressed. Why do the wicked renounce God, and say in their hearts, "You will not call us to account"? But you do see! Indeed you note trouble and grief that you may take it into your hands; the helpless commit themselves to you; you have been the helper of the orphan.* True, I never renounced God, but I never considered God truly before believing in Christ. Now I'm taken aback. Why would I deny a greater judgment than that of man exists in all of Creation? I'd ask this now, but 33 years passed before I woke up to my blindness.

Now, my task and burden beyond the wisdom of righteous confession, is also to remember and honor the blindness of those about me. This, too, is another form of violence I have often failed to mitigate in the call upon me to be generous of spirit to those in need. I was warned from long ago: *You have a tendency to self-righteous anger that is not serving you in the Lord.* Boy was it true. I've stumbled on this one sin so many times.

This was the sin of the Pharisees. One of their sins, anyway. It was especially heinous in God's sight to be teachers of the law, representatives of the burden of God's judgment and wisdom in living, and then to exercise that authority selfishly by laying a heavy burden on the backs of those they were called to guide and lift for their well-being. The peoples were accounted as sheep in need of a shepherd.

The scribes and teachers were appointed shepherds, a tremendous calling; but, they stood guilty of burdening and leading those sheep to death. There were some times that I forsook opportunities to extend the love of God to those who had never experienced what I was blessed to know despite my unworthiness to receive such blessing.

Of all these violences I've been guilty. In my personal frustrations and passion of convictions about what's right, I have struggled especially in my temperament to steward the gift of God's grace and wisdom in how I represent Him to those around me. Each sin is a violence I am called to submit to the way of peace He purchased in His body broken and blood shed to cover me. This was His love towards me in the face of His expectation of my soul to love others bearing His image.

This is honor: to love in peace, forsaking violence while pursuing the highest integrity always. And this is my failure in claiming to be a Christian when I go to church like everyone else: my self-righteous violence. At least, this understanding is the best I have managed to reach into so far. Who knows what else may become clearer to me over time.

Let Faith Arise

L AST NIGHT, I attended my regular women's Bible study, and an interesting thing occurred. I had a chance to share a praise song I'd been listening to earlier in the day with the group of twenty or so women. The song was titled "Reckless" and it describes the reckless love of God. *I couldn't earn it, I don't deserve it, yet You give Yourself away, Oh the overwhelming, never-ending reckless love of God.*

The singer is this beautiful, young, passionate woman lost in her love for the Lord. It is a stunning sight to see. I long for a love I once knew as I watch her zeal and yearning for God. I've known this love. I've known this passion. I've known what it is to be wrenched with desire for the One who loved me in ways I never imagined were possible in life. I never knew the love I knew in Him.

How did I ever get this far away from the love I started with? How did it ever get so defiled, so insecure, so lost? Because I've repented again and again and I've fasted just as much. To say I've tried to earn love is an understatement. Nonetheless, last night I listened closely to these lyrics about a relentless God who does not give up on you despite your shortcoming and straying. He leaves the 99 righteous sheep to pursue the one that strays and loses her way.

As I was listening, I reflected on this one night that I was desperately headed to the drug store to buy a cheap box of wine with my remaining laundry quarters. I felt so stupid faced with the wall of options when I got there. Running after a dead end in misery. Alcoholic even if I didn't drink too often—I still managed to stretch those quarters every chance I got in that season of depression. I turned around, forsaking my intention for cough drops instead. Walking home, I sensed His presence. I felt so terrible. Here He was, the glorious and beloved One—the very King of the Universe, and He's chasing me around a shopping strip for being a reckless idiot. I felt bad to put Him on the run after me, His stupid straying 38 year old sheep.

After we finished listening to the song, the leader of our ladies group declared that she felt blessed to see me worshipping. These women have born witness to my struggle. They know my conflict, strife, and insecurity in the Lord. This leader of ours was so patient with me. She insisted she spent three years early in her faith walk getting saved every Sunday and Wednesday at church, that deep was her insecurity in her salvation. So, her word to me was encouraging—that she would feel uplifted by my worship? Wow, talk about loving me.

What people are the children of the Lord. They amaze me in their kindness and love, their generosity. He is amazing. The work of His Spirit is amazing. Oh, how I long for reconciliation—not just for blessing sake, for relief from the heavy weight of justice; but, also for the love and zeal for God I once knew to anchor my life and drive me forward in a life of meaning, gravity, and joy.

This same woman sent a text today with a prayer and scripture that sums up my need and heart. In the Old Testament, King David commit a rather grave sin that many hold to when in need of hope in their own lives. He commit adultery with this married woman named Bathsheba, and she got pregnant. He then sent her husband to battle in the front lines of war to cover his crime.

The Lord took that child, but eventually they came to bear King Solomon in time. David declared his plea for forgiveness of his sin in the oft cited and famed Psalm 51. In this text message, our group leader sent me verses 10-12: *Create in me a clean heart, O God, and renew a steadfast spirit within me. Do not cast me away from your presence, and do not take your Holy Spirit from me. Restore me to the joy of Your salvation, and uphold me by Your generous Spirit.*

I've already known what it is to be cast away and to lose the Holy Spirit. It is horrible. I wouldn't wish it on any believer and would but hope to warn others as this end of my personal account strives to detail for the reader. It's hopeful to imagine that a King guilty of such a crime was actually restored in due time.

As I jotted this verse in my journal, I suddenly recalled a recent morning that I sat with the Bible searching my stand before God out of the scriptures. I was crushed. Every scripture leveled any hope I could hold onto. It was so demoralizing and weighty. I read Isaiah 53 about the Lord's sacrifice. Then, I heard an angel say, *Hold onto Isaiah 54. That chapter is for you.*

I'd completely forgotten this word of encouragement in all my disheartened woes. So, this afternoon I got out Isaiah 54 and read it.Wow. There couldn't be a more apt stretch of speech that addresses my current circumstance and need to reach into even a spark of faith that is actually well-founded. Through faith in this chapter, I could begin to hope on a dream.

It starts out stating, *Sing, O barren one who did not bear; you who have not been in labor! For the children of the desolate woman will be more than the children of her that is married, says the LORD.* Considering I literally reflected the other day on the fact that I just turned 40 and have never married or had any children but rather have passed that window concerned of my relationship to God and of my soul and purpose, this verse was rather accurate.

As I walked down the trail that day, I decided: *It's ok with me, I have no regrets.* Suddenly, I sensed the Lord's affirmation. He was pleased in this statement and decision in me. It was somehow a good thing, this measure of spontaneous self-ownership. He showed me that He takes pleasure in that aspect: *owning myself.* How strange, I thought. Ooook. I've often been conflicted about having a family and children, but it's passed now, and I myself felt a bit taken aback by my sudden acceptance and ownership. So there was this odd event recently.

Isaiah 54 goes on to declare in verse 4: *Do not fear, for you will not be ashamed; do not be discouraged, for you will not suffer disgrace; for you will forget the shame of your youth, and the disgrace of your widowhood you will remember no more. 5 For your Maker is your husband, the LORD of hosts is his name; the Holy One of Israel is your Redeemer, the God of the whole earth he is called.*

This reality is absolutely astounding to me. God Almighty. My Husband, just as I had sought out, but heavens He is a tough husband to measure up to in the weakness of my humanity. Verse 6 goes on to state, *For the LORD has called you like a wife forsaken and grieved in spirit, like the wife of a man's youth when she is cast off, says your God. 7 For a brief moment I abandoned you, but with great compassion I will gather you. 8 In overflowing wrath for a moment I hid my face from you, but with everlasting love I will have compassion on you, says the LORD, your Redeemer.* Wow. This is my precise hope. The scriptures never cease to amaze me. Who could even conceive or fathom such speech as this? It is beyond the imagination of man, to me. I can't begin to question the divine nature and source of such words as these.

Comparing this pardon to the days of Noah when the Lord vowed never to make an end of man in such a way again, He states in 54: 9-10, *...so I have sworn that I will not be angry with you and will not rebuke you. For the mountains may depart and the hills be removed, but my steadfast love shall not depart from you, and my covenant of peace shall not be removed, says the LORD, who has compassion on you.*

For each sin that brings to mind the vision of my God seated in perfect righteousness upon His throne, angry with me, staunch in a determined justice—how I long for this verse to supersede in a miraculous and sovereign will to pardon me with determined kindness and love.

I can't understand what I'm being put through. For as much violence as I'm guilty of committing, I endure a tremendous amount of mental violence with the expectation of forbearing obedience to a strict and stringent standard with little, albeit some measure yet still of love or approval to balance the load. I often reason my own worth down just to be able to obey properly, lecturing myself: *Don't forget, you deserve this. You commit the sins. You can't complain of being shamed and humiliated. You should've thought twice before you ever sinned.* And so on.

One night, I lay there on my bed and heard my heart accept it's reality in the effort to submit in supposed humility to this treatment: *I don't deserve love.* Then, I felt His grief, as though this wasn't true, but was actually a lie my heart was forced to accept in tortured submission. So, I sat reflecting: *Then, I DO deserve love?* Like some novel epiphany in this stream of hatred and worthlessness.

So, that's why I keep pleading, please just forgive me, love me? Why can't He just love me? If some part of me is worth loving, why not just love all of me? Despite being denied, I keep asking the same questions like a stubborn child tugging at His robe sleeve. Hey! What's up, Lord?! Love me already!!! Pleeeeaaase....

His promise to this barren, forsaken wife being forgiven forever goes on in verses 1-14: *O afflicted one, storm-tossed, and not comforted, I am about to set your stones in antimony, and lay your foundations with sapphires. I will make your pinnacles of rubies, your gates of jewels, and all your walls of precious stones... In righteousness you shall be established; you shall be far from oppression, for you shall not fear; and from terror, for it shall not come near you.*

This book began with my experience of nameless fear and terror afflicting me. I came to understand this later in terms of my fidelity to the Spirit. Perfect love casts out fear, true. But, one is perfected in love by cleansing and purifying oneself in the Spirit of truth and pursuing the Spirit's will walking in the light, practicing peace, mercy, and divine love. In a liberal, worldly walk you're not being perfected in love necessarily. So this was, I reasoned, why I struggled with fear. Fear has to do with punishment, merited by one who is not in the light due to sin.

Of course, at one point, a deliverance minister actually battled and cast away a "spirit of fear and intimidation." So, it's likely I was demonized, too. There is also the strange and somewhat unique experience I've endured in terms of the duality of good and evil within me. I was warned early on that I had a "constant presence of evil" that was "not of the Lord." This reality challenged me greatly.

And so, we come to the end of Isaiah 54 in verses 15-17:

> *If anyone stirs up strife, it is not from me; whoever stirs up strife with you shall fall because of you. See it is I who have created the smith who blows the fire of coals, and produces a weapon fit for its purpose; I have also created the ravager to destroy. No weapon that is fashioned against you shall prosper, and you shall confute every tongue that rises against you in judgment. This is the heritage of the servants of the LORD and their vindication from me, says the LORD.*

So, to fathom an angel actually gave me this chapter of scripture as a hope to hold onto in the face of the crushing judgment the rest of the Bible wielded against my reality before the Just Judge, well, that's just Awesome. That would actually be the only hope worth it's salt, literally. That hope could actually found a faith worthy. From this ash heap of a human being and story of faith's demise, it would take such a miracle as the pardon granted in this chapter to actually redeem love and life from my mess. In this miracle of pardon, faith could arise for me after all.

Being Whole

A YEAR AGO TODAY I had a very interesting experience. After a few years of disturbed sleep, rough awakenings, and tormented days, I woke up this particular morning to a dark, living black silence in my mind that was the equivalent of a sunny day for being 4am. From this lovely, luscious blackness, I climbed out of bed, walked into my closet and got dressed ever so naturally. If something so banal as getting dressed first thing in the morning could be a poised event, it sure was on this day.

I looked at myself in the mirror. I not only felt poised as I'd never before been so self-possessed, but I felt like—*that's so me. I feel so very me. In fact, I've never felt so very me and what's strange is: I like it. I like me. I am really wonderful.* Wow. What have I been thinking all my life? I'm an awful person, apparently. Why on earth is this some kind of epiphany all of a sudden? And why is it a *feeling*?

It's not only a feeling. I feel happy to see a friend after a long time. I feel frustrated by the demonic. I feel comforted by my cat. I feel a lot of things. But this feeling had a different location. The soul is a nebulous thing and perhaps a more nebulous place. This feeling had it's residence without doubt in my soul. It was rather otherworldly.

Everything I chose and did was done with this delicious decisiveness, a knowing and doing that fit me like the clothing I chose to wear. Never had I known this. Always sorting, sifting, struggling to decide—make the right choice from the menu item to the career to the next priority and so on. Big, small, doesn't matter. Most of the time I'm pleased with my plate spinning. But, I never knew this other way of being until this odd morning.

I was informed by angels as I headed to Starbucks in the dark, *the feeling you're having is called "wholeness." You've been made whole in your soul.* Well, heavens, no kidding! I've apparently been fragmented or shattered the rest of my life. I'd heard of people "being made whole" by the Lord's healing love and work. I always wondered what that was anyway. It's the best thing ever. If only I could make it happen again.

As I got in line and considered my normal order—I decided, you know, the Lord doesn't want me to drink coffee. I ordered a green tea decisively, contented to make a different choice. I wore my new decision like the outfit, again. I sat in an armchair listening to the ambient music—cosmic sounding electronic music like I used to listen to in my twenties.

I reminisced as my mind considered my life and it's history with a sense of settled acceptance and satisfaction. It seemed the starry universe was the implicit backdrop to all this reflecting. I felt like I was casually hanging out with God. Not a "Father," necessarily, but rather a gigantic never-ending consciousness that occupied every distance and light I could see. I wrote down in my journal a phrase I kept speaking in tongues to myself: *may iti asa.* I understood it to mean: *and I, too, was.*

Like, the great I Am decided to try life as me, a spark amongst many who also were. Truly, a strange sensation all of this was. I felt zero judgment. In fact, it didn't seem to matter that I was a person on earth. I was just as contented to sort of dance around in the stars to that music free from bodily constraints. And I wasn't high. Just sober and whole. I see why people seem to discover that "healing" is often found in self-acceptance.

As novel and transformative as that gift of a morning was to me, I was later stumbled by early afternoon, and subsequently crushed by evening. A relationship run-in and an employment concern seemed sufficient obstacles to destroy this beautiful experience. I've not known it since that day. The day was marked on this account and now it's the anniversary of my special healing morning.

Because of this experience, I know one thing—it's possible. God is able to accomplish this feat in a moment's notice by His sovereign will. I never prayed or fasted or received prayer or learned lessons—nothing. I did absolutely nothing to bring it about. I had no warning or even explanation for why this happened, or why it ended. It just came and went and became a testament of the potential in me for wholeness. It also highlights the apparent fact that the trouble and instability I struggle against is an extension, at least in part, of a fractured soul.

As I write, I sense again the same pleasure in self-acceptance as I did before in my reflection about not regretting my choice to stay single. Another oddity. I can't get past shame and the justice of it's possible exposure on account of sins against grace; yet, it seems the same God that I'm struggling to reconcile myself to is pleased that I shouldn't regret my life? That I should like myself? That I shouldn't self-deprecate? That I should know that I do deserve love?

What an absolutely bizarre insanity is it that I should be sandwiched between a holy justice pressing down upon my sins and my past; and yet, the same King seems to somehow be alongside me as some strange kind of soul-sojourner pointing me to these essential sorts of lessons about self, worth, and purpose in life.

Jesus is often described as God in the flesh. He left His eternal throne to take up the form of a babe born in so humble a home as a manger. New age people say he was a sage reincarnated. I believe He incarnated from His throne. I also believe I came from heaven somehow. I don't know what to say about incarnation. It's just a deep intuition. The day I commit to the Lord, I knew He was my *origin,* my home— I came from Him. My Hope would be to return to Him after I die.

If that's my Hope, then judgment is no small reality to fathom; yet, there is something about this dichotomy between the Jesus I see in my mind's eye occupying an unimaginably intimidating throne and the one that seems to disclose pleasure in my forsaking regrets. The mystery from the start of this journey comes to mind also—the night I ate the fancy dinner and sank into the pit from so deep a remorse over my past and the sins against the Lord. As I sank, I recall the warning that regret itself was a sin that hurt and offended Him.

In fact, I couldn't even remember the other sins. I just sank into black mire. All I remembered on the way down was this word about regret, and of course, the morning afterward warned me: *See, you are loved. Trust in your Father. He is greater than your sins.* What an odd recollection and anniversary in light of my struggle of recent in these last couple of months.

Today, I am holding onto a word I received a week ago on my way to visit a prophetess who ministered to the ladies in our Bible study group. Although I didn't complete the fast the Lord asked of me in the days prior to our visit, I was warned by my angels on the way to seeing her, *Have faith—praise is your key.*

The woman who hosted this prophetess and our visits was a woman that I particularly looked up to and admired in our group. She described casting demons out of her daughter. Her prayers were always so powerful, so obviously attuned to the Spirit—His very words. I feel like I can recognize His words because they are so distinct and powerful. This was the same woman who confessed that the Holy Spirit fell on her at church a couple of weeks prior and told her to tell me that God loves me and to stop fasting.

I was shocked because that was exactly how I felt and what I felt I needed so badly. To hear it confirmed miraculously in someone whose faith I trusted meant a lot to me. The Lord and the Spirit are such a strange mystery. Especially when it comes to His wisdom in prayer and intercession. I've consistently noticed that the prayers that affected me miraculously were the prayers that He asked someone to pray for me and often that person had suffered similarly in some way.

The same was true for me. The prayers that I was asked to pray and that seemed to produce miraculous fruit in someone's life were prayers that acknowledged a link of mutuality in suffering, a wisdom of suffering and sacrifice. It seemed in some instances that to be worthy to lift a prayer for another person's needs involves experience, not just right standing in the King.

It's really neat to consider this intercessory weave that brings people to cover each other's needs. This is a way of Love covering sin that isn't quite the same as being kind and forgiving and uplifting towards someone. To lend your hope and heart and sacrifice on someone's account because you have rights to pray against their pain, that's saying a lot about the Lord's justice schemes and how powerful man has the potential to be in impacting another person's lot.

I imagine all these fractured souls yet to be made whole locking into one and another at various turns of life. Like, so many broken pieces searching for help, searching for purpose, place, and self—finding one's spot in the confusion of seaming together the past and building a better future. Maybe I'm just hoping there's a good reason I've suffered and I only knew that "wholeness" for one day. I'm often assured, once God pulls you through this, you'll be prepared to help others.

I really, really hope so. Oh, how I want to feel whole again.

Through the Looking Glass

I F MAKING ONE'S soul whole is the healing work of God to accomplish, it's also the work of psychologists and doctors dedicated to helping people cope with trauma. People are God's instruments of love and healing a lot of the time—vessels for His spirit to work through. But the thing is, the person need not believe or relate to God for them to be used by God, loved by God.

Despite that belief, I want to point out that it is only the born again believer that is filled with the Holy Spirit and guided by Him "into all truth." This is a biblical reality shared in the book of John. In chapter 3, Jesus shares with a Pharisee named Nicodemus with regard to the miracles He was doing: *Very truly I tell you, no one can see the kingdom of God without being born from above.*

This "born again" reality is what it is to be "filled with the Holy Spirit." Later in chapter 14, Jesus states that on the believer's behalf, *I will ask the Father, and he will give you another Advocate, to be with you forever. This is the Spirit of truth, [the Holy Spirit], whom the world cannot receive, because it neither sees him nor knows him. You know him, because he abides in you, and he will be in you.* This is a key distinction between believers filled with the Holy Spirit and unbelievers that may yet be in service to the love of God in their own spirit that I don't want this chapter to neglect, despite the insights I hope to share.

That said, in the realm of church, there is talk of believers and non-believers, of the Kingdom and the World. It took me so long to distinguish these and understand their differences that it was a novel discovery at CFNI when my trouble came together in the auditorium one day: *Ah! There is a*

"Kingdom" in the World AND a "World" in the Kingdom! That's where I got confused and that epiphany cleared it up for me instantly.

Day after day, we students gathered in that auditorium prepared to learn more about the scriptures, more about the history of theology, and more about such specialized matters of the present day as the work and movement of God's angelic hosts. We were obviously in and of the Kingdom. We dealt with Kingdom matters, and we were Kingdom people. Much as I was excited to be immersed in this place entirely devoted to the object of my love and worship, I was often at odds with my unbelieving immediate family.

I have a small, intimate family that has stayed committed to each other's lives all my life. My parents never divorced, despite any challenges over the years, standing on the commitment they claimed marriage to be—uncompromising. My baby sister always buffered the blows of my rebellion and risk-taking against my parents' marriage bond. They seemed consistently at odds about how to deal with me.

For example, from a very young age, I decided I really liked the strange gory body, and I wanted to be a doctor. Eventually, I found the brain fascinating and did well in AP science and decided I wanted to be neuroscientist. After 3 years of premed, I decided my doubts about medicine were so deep that I was following through with marrying the wrong man just because it was the day before the wedding (the year of taking the MCAT). That's no reason to marry the wrong career.

So, I turned course. I was undeclared in my major and decided to not only renounce medicine but also to declare a major in studio art. I also decided to chop off my hair in a boy cut and dye it red (which came out more of a magenta, of course). Then, I came home to my poor parents and informed their eyes and ears of all my decisions. I was a junior in college, twenty years old, and a bit overdue for a rebellion that was ever a true part of myself but sure would have been better born out in high school. Anyway, they were really lovely people in receiving all this.

Yes, they immediately dyed my hair back, horrified of what had become of their "good" daughter. Ultimately, my parents accepted my decision to major in art and renounce medicine. They always supported me without judgment. In high school, they never pressured me to be a doctor. Instead, they defended my academic ambition that seemed to make of their teenager a bit of a recluse snob who refused to party with the other kids.

My blessed parents subsequently fielded naked portrait drawings from that year on with no complaint but for innocent shock at the normal practices of art school. Look what they do, these people these days. Having accrued many psych classes pursuing my neuroscience dream, I dual majored in Psychology. After graduating, I used this degree to work with three developmentally disabled women for a couple of years as a case manager while I did artsy things. I painted and participated in this annual indie film festival with the art friends I had made in school.

Eventually, I ended up back with my parents and searched out my next chapter. For two years, I managed to pass over a postcard of the Last Supper on my wall without taking note of this Jesus fellow. In that time, I got so "crazy" that at one point, I insisted that the devil was in our house and pleaded with my father, in my unwitting and intrinsic Fear of the Lord— *do you believe in Judgment Day?* He said, "I don't know. Are you ok?" Well, that answer and question didn't help me with my fear. I was terrified. Without saying anything, I ended up in my first psychiatric hospitalization for five days. I came out of this stay promising, of all things, to straighten my life out and become a family therapist.

Somehow that promise was going to keep me from the pit of hell. There was plenty of God and Judgment and Hell that I lived through and considered, but no Jesus. Of course, some eight years later, I finally took note of Jesus and only Jesus. Now, I am rather amazed at the hiding magic acts of the Lord, but for my own ignorance. Talk about veiling His reality from my awareness.

Hide and seek, this King played my life in absolute mercy for the sake of my future. He truly was so kind as to veil Himself and extend the hope of my salvation a bit down the line when I'd be more established in my life professionally, more mature as a person, and I imagine He may have considered, more prepared to honor His grace for goodness sake. He gave me almost another decade to develop. He is truly *so* good.

Now, I have to deal with this understanding in the face of my negligence. Despite that grace I see now, I've been a let down. So many sacrifices for the "hope of glory" for me, and I managed to sin against them to the point that I'm pleading another salvation over my hopes for a future. But, I'm an old forty years now, not an ignorant and naïve 25 or 33. Not so sweet anymore.

Anyway, at the time, at 25, the promise to become a counselor turned into applications to anthropology and art education graduate programs. My father supported me despite insisting that I consider a practical path like becoming a pharmacist. They make a nice $70,000 after a few years of schooling. To me, my work had to be aligned with my passion. He accepted and supported me again.

He and my sister read all my application essays and gave me feedback. He helped me compile my application packets. He reasoned with me about different programs. He encouraged me not to give up when I faced any setbacks. He hoped on that Harvard rejection letter as he opened it, genuinely believing in his child.

On the other end, my mother picked my despair-ridden, rock-bottom-hitting soul off the floor of the pits morning after morning following that hospital stint. I wondered from where this woman managed her sheer chutzpah to face being alive with such utter bravado and zeal in the face of such deep depression.

My mom has fought depression, epilepsy, pain, prejudice, and all manners of obstacles in this beautiful spirit of resilience. I always admired her will to live. And in this season of my life, she instilled it in me—dragging me up from my low to believe on my future again. Over time, I submit about five applications. I was accepted to both anthropology and art education with scholarships at the school I ended up enrolling in. All with the help of my family.

Despite my parents natural concern for my efforts to become an art teacher anthropologist, they eventually took pride in my success when I got hired at the high school. They saw a happy, productive, self-sufficient young woman of a daughter that seemed to please her supervisors, coworkers, and students. I fulfilled their hopes ultimately—in my own dream, not as a pharmacist. They didn't complain, like good parents. Maybe I didn't make as handsome an income, but their desire for my well-being was satisfied.

My life as a teacher was almost alright. Knowing what I know now, I would have lived a responsible life of gratitude for the great burden and gift of teaching teenagers. At the time, I just extended my grad school ethic into working days that became a double life. I figured I was an average teacher in many ways. After getting saved, I saw things very, very differently. I changed, my lessons changed, my life's purpose changed.

My leaving the classroom really disturbed my family. My parents insisted that I pursue night classes and continue teaching until I knew I was certain about enrolling in another degree program. They didn't want me to give up such a good job and take such a chance with my life. They were weary of my religiosity as I'd become so passionate and single-minded about my God. They didn't trust all of it.

They weren't necessarily right, and I wasn't necessarily wrong. I just wasn't mature enough to float the risks I took down what eventually became river rapids. I folded. I wasn't well founded because I'd taken liberties along the way. The moral of this reflection though is that for each step of blind faith I took away from that successful life I once knew, my family was along for the ride, peering over the fence of the Kingdom/World divide.

If I was less of a person to boast of my recent intellectual discoveries in studying scripture and more a person to quietly do community service while holding side jobs and studying for my new program, perhaps my case to pursue the King so blindly risking all would have sat with a greater peace in my parents than it did. I'd be living it out instead of preaching what was not under my feet.

Before enrolling at CFNI, I was appalled at my father's faithlessness. What do you mean you don't see how I'm spending my money on a ministry school? He's God! If it's His will, He will provide, Dad! He has all the money in the world. He's not going to call me into something and then leave me stranded. Don't you get it? Ugh. My father. So rude to my God. Such an offense.

Now, I remember my poor Dad trying to make sense of my decisions. He'd spent all his life calculating risks to invest his earnings for our family and my welfare. Now, he's too stupid to respect my God properly. Naturally, I'm not the problem. I'm not too stupid for anything in the middle of all this confusion. So, I invested the last of my savings into CFNI to my father's concern.

My mom, crazy woman, was concerned about all my torment and insisted she wanted me to come home and get psychiatric help. She pleaded with me to come to Houston and forego the schooling at CFNI. I prayed about it, releasing my heart's desire to go to CFNI in the event that the Lord willed for me to move to Houston. I felt the door opening to CFNI was in God's blessing, so I accepted. This crushed my Mom's hopes to fix my torments, which had worsened just before my leaving.

On top of all that, CFNI is a spirit-filled school so they embrace and celebrate not only daily worship, but miracles and destinies and all the big magical stuff of faith that's scary from the outside unless, I imagine, you know it as a reality in the life of someone you trust. So, my family was concerned I might be getting sucked into a cult when I was already demonized as it was. She just wanted medicine to help her child like it did the last time she went "crazy." Never mind, coming home speaking in tongues did nothing to help any of this.

In my effort to mitigate my family's concerns I spent time researching cults. I learned quite a bit about poorly founded ministries that rise on good intent and fall in eventual corruption. I felt really informed. I was glad I couldn't find any negative commentary about CFNI. I was worried that perhaps there was information online I never bothered to search before enrolling that was worrying my family. This wasn't the case. I love that school and wish it the best and would be happy for anyone blessed to go there. Personally, I should be so blessed I ever was a student there.

Despite all this, it was a tough split—my embrace of that particular step of faith. I found that the Lord was not pleased in my cult researching. I wasn't supposed to try to understand their perspective by learning things that weren't my concern and were not of the light. My mind was steeped in all kinds of darkness spawned of this research. This was not the way to go.

I felt bound though. I didn't really know how else to honor them. I kept sinning. We'd get into arguments, and I'd realize they were actually extending the love of the Lord to me better than I'd managed to do my job as a Christian towards them. The Lord was more pleased in their loving concern, so I strove to honor them by seeking empathic understanding to help me be more humble and compassionate. This was like the spiritual equivalent of cheating.

It was a cheat sheet for my heart to do it's job in the Lord decently. This one time I was on the phone with my sister, and I was suddenly able to see through her wounded love in our misunderstanding. In that momentary insight, I was naturally able to honor her in my reaction to our conflict as I felt it was my duty in the Lord. I was actually pleasing to Him that time. But, this incident and it's nature stuck out on the whole. I could only credit His Spirit with the ability to see my sister truly anyway.

I felt frustrated as it seemed God rewarded their love towards me in empathy while my efforts to defend the calling on me as a Christian that made no sense to them were sinful and displeasing. Meanwhile, standing against "religiousity," my mom would post quotes on Facebook saying:

"You don't need religion, you need empathy." I got even more frustrated. As if I wouldn't love to just empathize? Unfortunately, it wasn't that simple.

Seeking empathy as a tool was not necessarily a legitimate avenue of reconciliation for me in God's expectations of me, not of my family. I suppose the Lord expected me to pray. If I'd been more disciplined, sacrificial, and obedient, I believe His Spirit would have revealed more moments to me like that time with my sister, to mitigate the conflict and confusion to His pleasure. As it stood, I was bailing water with whatever means I could manage or figure out.

This dynamic with my family and friends was one example of this "World in the Kingdom" observation. Here I was, supposedly a child of the Kingdom, yet drowning in my efforts, striving in the ways of the World, instead of the light of the Spirit—as I was called to reflect to the World. Just because they weren't believers didn't mean they weren't better reflections of the Kingdom of God than I was, spending my savings at a ministry school. And so what? What does it amount to anyway? Ultimately, Christians are human, ever being matured through the same humanity into the image of their Savior. And humans reflect the Kingdom in so far as there is still a Christ loving them and at work in love through them in the World.

If I could embody this awareness more deeply somehow, I think I'd be a more understanding and wise person in situations of conflict that involve confusion in care and love misunderstood. I hope it sinks in until I'm a bit less blind of another person's blind, never mind my own blindness ever unfolding in my trials and errors over time. Ay, to see through the through the through. Someday, better and better, hopefully.

I Am...

I N Exodus 3:14, God sent Moses back to the Israelites with word from "I Am." Moses asked Him what to tell them if they should question him about His name. So, God said to Moses, *"I AM WHO I AM."* Then He said, *"Thus you shall say to the Israelites, 'I AM has sent me to you."* For His purposes, God was satisfied to deny any name but that He is, God. I take this to mean, He owes me no name. He exists as God, and that's all I need to know.

In His goodness, the Lord is known for having many names that characterize His many attributes. Jehovah Rapha, for example, means the Lord Our Healer. Or, Jehovah Jireh means the Lord Our Provider. Amongst the many names, this story in Exodus stands out to me because it is the root of identity. If I say, "I am," there is a definition to follow because whatever I am, I'm not God.

I may be of God, like God in some ways, hoping to be more like God, made in His image; but, I'm always something else depending on what follows those two key words. For example, I like to drink and have struggled with abusing alcohol at times. At some points, I've been sucked into it's addictive grip, and it would have been fair enough for me to say, "I am an alcoholic."

I've heard some people describe their reasoning about this particular term. Does your friend or husband or whomever drink everyday? No. Then, he's not an alcoholic. Does he drink first thing in the morning? No. Then, he's not an alcoholic. The encouragement is meant to save that person from qualifying legitimately for this identity. By the time they qualify according to whoever's standard, then they're an alcoholic.

It's a big deal. To suddenly qualify and become something, to acquire an entire identity. On this one account, a person may run from identifying, to their own detriment. Perhaps all the supports and steps associated with claiming the identity would save this person's life, but they refuse to their harm, choosing to stay in denial of their reality. This identification step in AA stares that denial down and steps onto the road of overcoming death in taking personal responsibility.

I get all that. It makes sense. I wouldn't speak against it for so many reasons. Yet, there is a certain power to laying claim to the words that follow "I am" in one's life, and I'm interested in understanding the nature of this transaction better. So, I want to use this chapter to try to unpack this loaded topic.

I've come to consider this today due to my personal frustration feeling stuck spiritually. I desire this dream vision laid before me. I desire a God that receives my simple repentance and grants me the opportunity to pursue such a path of service on account of my intention's purity, my motivation's goodness, and the hope of redemption. I'm confronted with a God who is challenging me to realize that He may want as much for me in His own goodness, but I'm no child and He's expecting more sacrificial penance and respect for His just nature and judgment than I'm living out. He's not pleased, and I'm not getting the hope of my wish until I change.

My changing runs into my rebellion. I resist this call to fast because of my history with fasting. I've grown frustrated and demoralized trying to prove myself in the face of such shame and failure. Yet, I've been warned by angels that this "sex trafficking" that is my personal trial is better than actually being trafficked, stuck in kidnapped bondage being sexually abused by filthy men. I agree. But, my suffering is my own experience to bear and it isn't without the merit of it's own sympathy, too. This, especially when I'm trying to discern the truth and how to honor it for the sake of a good hope and future. For salvation's sake, especially and then for the "hope of glory."

So, in the face of this, I took note one day this summer when something different and unusual happened that struck me. There I was standing in my kitchen by the counter when I suddenly felt my heart submit accepting as truth the statement "I AM a ...." It was absurd and unacceptable. By the time my heart's accepting this as true, it's been steamrolled in it for so long and cornered in failed calls to obey for so long, that that particular rampart just fell over. Some nameless dam broke and just came to agree with the "enemy." I'm not supposed to claim such an identity for myself, nor would I. Who would?

I'm more likely to say something like I actually said to myself this last summer: *I am a failure.* Well, compared to the enemy's victory above, failure is a pretty kind term. Never mind it's really nice, it's also pretty accurate to reality. So, in terms of personal responsibility, and self-ownership, you'd think this is a humble moment of realization and self-acceptance. I wasn't giving up on the present or the future on this account, by the way. I was actually plugging away at building as much a life back as I could manage. But, one afternoon, as I considered my past few years and all the damage and missed windows for redemption, I came to this conclusion.

Then, out of nowhere I sensed God's grief at my realization— "failure" was a statement He didn't seem pleased I should have thought or accepted of myself. It was as though it wasn't fair towards me in His eyes. It wasn't accurate to Him. So, I was left wondering, what on earth? You mean to tell me, Life and the Universe and Existence and All the Mystery therein: to Him, I am *not* a failure? Strrraaange. How is that possible? It's a blatant fact if ever one could validate a matter as such. I could've sworn I was just being humble and true. What gives? If He doesn't see me that way, then how does He see me? Now, I hear in my heart: *Innocent.* Great.

In the face of this divine disagreement, even to this day, I have no good answers. When I thought this, I really would have struggled to see my life differently; and, I was more than ok with that. So, I've failed. Ok. Now, what can I do with what's in front of me, at my disposal, to change my lot for the better despite my failures? If I accept and learn, perhaps I could move forward for the better. Anyway, surely others have insights I can't come up with that might help me.

I think back to so much Christian-talk when I first converted. The key to succeeding in the battle against the devil seemed to consistently rest upon "knowing who you are in Christ." I came to understand this subject of identity was important, but I never quite got it. It's a big part of just about every deliverance book I've read. It's key to getting free of demons, addiction, strife, etc.

In fact, it's the key to claiming your legal rights in Christ as a believer and child of God. It's a lot like knowing your rights as a citizen before the law in the world. It just happens to be a divine courtroom. So, the prosecuting attorney, the devil, wants you to remain ignorant of these rights so you don't exercise them correctly.Then, he's free to rob you. God is always working to redeem, as your defender. So, the devil's ability to rob is standing against a loving and righteous judge. Yet, God expects you to learn and claim your place proactively, to grow in wisdom and understanding—to withstand the wiles of the devil in battle.

So, there's these long scripture lists that speak to what God sees in you, not what the devil sees. The devil sees an alcoholic. If you're down enough in your own esteem given the circumstance confronting your soul, you may just come to agree with the devil and not God. God's saying something like, *Hey, I know it's tough now, but I died for you—my son, my child, my beloved—not just, "an alcoholic." See yourself in the value you hold for Me, not Satan. He despises your soul. I cherish your soul. Put down the drink and rest on the hope of eternity with the One who loves you.*

Meanwhile, the bitter and evil devil would speak thoughts to the effect of: *You know what you are—a natural drinker. It's the good stuff isn't it? You can't deny your truth. You loved it from the time you first laid lips on it. Wasn't that last glass even better—it's gonna be ok now. You feel better. Everything's gonna be ok. You can fix it all once you're free, like you feel now.*

And so on. As one familiar with drinking like a drinker does, I don't actually think all those devil thoughts, but I might as well. They describe the consistent turn I take down the path that leaves me regretting it faster and faster. I'm trying to capture all this dynamic reality in the framework provided me from the Bible. Yet, this is my lived experience I must try to reconcile not just to the Bible, but also to the knowledge of God provided me by the Spirit, and then my own heart that is somehow distinct in all this.

I want to know the place of identity in this because there's some odd sort of power in accepting or declaring what and who one is in this life. I want to own that power and turn my whole lot around if I can manage it. This issue of I Am matters because my sense of self is such a part of my esteem which is such a part of my motivation, courage, and will. My choices end up affected, and I end up repentant when I could be victorious; or, I end up suffering consequences when I could be free.

God says choose who you will serve because you'll either be a slave of righteousness or sin. But, Love died to redeem "an alcoholic" to his unique and irreplaceable identity saved in grace. So, a part of the weaponry the believer must wield against Satan is scripture. As I just considered, Satan's hypothetically whispering into your defeated hopeless circumstance that you've always loved this, as you pour your third glass of wine, isn't it so good to you, so faithful, etc.

If that believer doesn't snap out of it and realize she's agreeing with the devil, she's headed towards the wrong suffering. The Bible wants her to be loaded with statements that counter these beliefs and choices: *I was fearfully and wonderfully made. In God, I have power, love, and a sound mind. I am the Lord's beloved and child. He has prepared for me a home and already secured my victory. I need to just seek refuge in the hope He's provided me because He's faithful to redeem me from the mess I'm trying to cover with a drink.*

I only wish I'd reasoned all this out these last two years. I'm reflecting on it now, but man did I live it differently. I backslid drinking repeatedly. I didn't have an identity issue with alcohol but to recognize I have a tendency and temperament unique to me that likes to drink. Biblically, alcohol was apparently intended to "cheer the heart" in the face of life's trial and burden, to help with health ailments on occasion and so on. Whether for good or bad, I don't think I can say I'm an alcoholic, in fairness. Yet, boy am I an alcoholic at root sometimes. I must cast off this identity for the hope of life, ultimately.

So, what am I? As of today, I've decided that ultimately and essentially, I'm Unworthy. I recently attended the writer's group I am a member of and sat as a reader of a chapter our leader was sharing detailing the Lord's crucifixion. All I kept thinking was: I. Am. A Wretch. Again and again. I hate it. I hate the cross. I am without doubt this much, a wretch. I have zero uncertainty of this identity. Before His cross, to say I'm unworthy is not strong enough by a lot. Words feel stupid and paltry, absolutely offensive. Useless.

I'm a wretch before my Savior, and I have no recourse save to plead: please look upon my goodness; please choose to value and magnify that which was ever light and love in me; please count me sufficient to merit security, dignity, and purpose in living a decent life of simple love and service; please be merciful towards my failure and shame; please allow me a chance to demonstrate my fidelity towards you in dignified love; please grant me trials that are different from what I've known withstanding the torments of demonic cursing; please release me from holy justice weighing my past sin and present "rebellion." *Please pardon me.*

Even more, I am not sinning to claim that I deserve love, despite being a wretch without question. I am not sinning to desire and deserve decency and purpose in the face of accusations. I deserve to be acknowledged for what is true and good and pure in me in the face of my faults and failures, even before holy sacrifice. I Am a Loving Person. I am a Hardworking Person. I am an Honest Person. I am a Patient Person.

I am someone who genuinely desires to accomplish her best personhood given the opportunity to grow and develop against her shortcomings and errors. I am someone who deserves Love. I deserve to Love and to grow more perfect in it before a Lord I have loved genuinely. And, I know I am true. As God is my witness, I Am Good, on the whole. If He chooses to look upon my good by the grace that ever suffered my evils for that very purpose, to magnify His generosity towards all that is good in me, I know : *I should be so blessed.* This self-accusation lingers undeniable as my every claim against His justice. I'm stuck with being entirely, utterly Wrong, despite myself.

So, ultimately, I pray for His mercy and grace upon me that I might actually bring Him glory in my goodness rather than in the vindication of His holy justice against me. I guess only time will speak to the results of my struggle and my case as I'm documenting it in the hopes that my honesty and sharing might speak to another and serve in some way for their good. So, in the end, all I Am is Alive and Hoping against hope for love and grace to win my salvation despite justice. I want mercy to triumph over judgment, for me.

A Chosen People

But you are a chosen people, a royal priesthood, a holy nation, God's special possession, that you may declare the praises of him who called you out of darkness into his wonderful light.

1 Peter 2:9

IT'S A DIFFICULT reality to face as a person: inclusion and exclusion. Yet, from grade school on, it is an undeniable part of life. Rejection and exile are likely some of the most painful emotions and realities to endure. In school and online, bullying leads many kids to depression and even suicide. Acceptance or rejection from opportunities like participating in sports or pursuing an education can make or break a life's dream. A good deal of the hatred at work in such dire matters as war and political strife is literally born of enmity between alliances identified with particular sides, inclusion and exclusion.

The Old Testament demonstrated exile to be a merciful, and yet, severe punishment in the justice of the law. Cain pleaded with the Lord who vowed he would succeed even in the face of his exile in the world. Cities of refuge were a provision for criminals granted asylum in the face of their exile from their home community. At the root of this matter, what could be more charged in a debate about the existence of God, Judgment, and the Afterlife, than the standards of inclusion in God's family of redemption? To be a Child of God. That is a tremendously difficult reality and identity to grapple with as a person, much less the consideration of eternity and destination.

Over these last two years, as the window of opportunity for me to break through into my destiny came and passed, I was hampered from truly embracing the confidence it would take to go forward in my struggle for faith that I am legitimately saved. My father helped me to seek counsel from a well-respected and very experienced and loving pastor here. Week after week, we hashed out the most challenging doctrine and life issues I was having. He continued to insist, "I see the love of God in you and the scripture confirms your salvation on this account." Well, in retrospect, I should have simply accepted this and let those grave scriptures be.

I never found salvation to be some generous promise in the Bible. There is a great deal of expectation in the scriptures and the reality of Judgment is not glossed over by any stretch. I say this after taking the time to find what others insisted was an overwhelming love and hope. Love and hope are there, too. But they have a standard and that standard is the highest there could be: holy. At one point, my counselor shared with me that this one book kept coming to mind in our sessions: Grace Abounding to the Chief of Sinners by John Bunyan. This man understood the gravity of the call to holiness in the scriptures. What a relief he was to me at the time!

He was a self-converted heathen from the 1600's in England. At some point in his life as a criminal, he took note of the light and love and joy of the Christians in his town. He started seeking them out on the periphery, observing them. Eventually, he decided to read their book and took to discerning the wisdom of good and evil in the Bible for himself. Over years, he sought to win the love of this God by reconciling his conscience and life to His standard of good. In due time, he was imprisoned for hosting study, worship, and praise in his home with other believers, against the law commanding worship by rote in the Church of England. During his thirteen years in prison, he penned over 60 books, "Grace" being the second.

He emerged as one of the most notable and powerfully impacting evangelists in history. In this book, he described being crushed by judgment before taking to the stage to preach to a crowd. During his preaching, he was imparted tremendous power. Then, as he walked off the stage, he was again crushed by judgment. I took heart. It seemed perhaps there was hope for me. Even now, remembering this, I feel more hope. At the time over a year ago, my counselor's assurances fell on ears that simply couldn't find security in them, even though I trusted the purity and truth of my own love for God. It simply wasn't sufficient.

I may have been partly wrong looking back. I do remember at one point the Holy Spirit asked me, "What about all the gifts you've been given?" He was referring to the various strengths and talents God's granted me. Why am I so faithless as to let them go to waste? I literally couldn't reconcile myself against the scriptures and in this standard my stand suffered in my frustration. Eventually I lost the Spirit's support and presence and power.

God was still faithful to place believers and community in my life, to give me an opportunity to stay grounded in some measure in my faith and perhaps have some soil in which to take root in my efforts to redeem what I once knew. Grace as this may have been, boy did I begin to suffer a battle with jealousy and envy. So many beautiful, bright daughters of the King. No better place in life than this. Truly, there is no greater compliment to one's being I could desire or hope upon. And I was surrounded by these beauty queens. The call upon my reality was to remain humble and submitted to my truth, to love and admire these women for all they embodied, and to continue diligently attending my own person, just as John Bunyan had done in the face of the bright Christians he admired.

Boy is that effort less clean when it's not laid out as a theoretic prescription in a nice, concise paragraph of reflection. Week after week of our giant ladies bible study left me demoralized. It didn't help that the book everyone was studying, slowly savoring each page's profound insight, was devoted to "the power of blessing." It's essential message was founded on Jesus' call to love and bless one's enemies. He encouraged listeners and aspiring disciples to consider the ways of the world in contrast to the values of heaven. Heaven's standard for love was far stiffer than typical earthly alliances would example. On earth, friends are naturally generous to friends. It's being generous to the stranger, or to the unworthy, that tax the natural inclination to share of one's self and possessions.

To extend the heart to love and bless the one who harms you or purposes evil against you— well, that's the ultimate generosity of spirit. In this day, to bear witness to the measure of generosity taking place in areas of the world suffering war and persecution is astounding. By the time your family members were torturously murdered before your sight and you end up seeking out the murderers to minister the love of Christ for the sake of their soul's salvation, well, that's loving the worst enemy life could conceive against your heart and soul.

There is no greater robbery of life than rape, torture, murder, such hatred and violence. Yet, the Christian brings to light the woman who has mercy on the unborn child of her rapist, the man who has mercy on the killer who fails in his effort to rob him of life, the child who stands before the end of his life as a martyr proclaiming his fidelity to Yeshua in undying love. It is in such stories that one hears of murderers changing heart to join Yeshua in love. They testify to the Christians that end up adopting and discipling them, "I never knew such a love existed." They are wowed and won over by this insane love. It turns everything in life other than It on it's head. So, this book we were studying was devoted to this concept of blessing one's enemy. You'd think for the essential nature of this principle, I would have benefited.

Unfortunately, each week I grew more and more disillusioned as I realized it's principles had never bore the fruit it promised for me in my life. Testimony after testimony insisted God was faithful to bless the blesser. If you'd just take the chance to extend yourself, He would show you how generously the one who blesses profits from their generosity. Well, I had spent years wishing and hoping to the bottom of myself against the devil, evil, and all manners of complexity and strife for my "enemies" to be blessed. I put that word in quotes because despite being warned by my angels to understand that this person who was traditionally a friend or family member was not my "friend" at the time—spiritually, they were opposing me in ways my naïveté was unable to understand.

The scriptures say that faith in Jesus will divide friends and family. In Luke 12:49-53 Jesus states:

> "I came to bring fire to the earth, and how I wish it were already kindled! I have a baptism with which to be baptized, and what stress I am under until it is completed! Do you think that I have come to bring peace to the earth? No, I tell you, but rather division! From now on five in one household will be divided, three against two and two against three; they will be divided: father against son and son against father, mother against daughter and daughter against mother, mother-in-law against her daughter-in-law and daughter-in-law against her mother-in-law."

How does this happen? Justice and Loyalty. There is this karmic rise and fall of favor and position that I've come to know and the effort to forgive across the strife grows strained. Love is loyal much as unity and peace are valued. There is the valor of an overcoming forgiveness like that being demonstrated in areas of war and persecution. Yet, there is also the defensive loyalty love demonstrates in vindicating injustice.

When someone wronged me or my purity or righteousness, they suffered. I suppose it was sin against the Lord's spirit in me or my alignment with His nature. Likewise, when I sinned against the purity, righteousness, or innocence in someone else, I suffered. Not surprising to suffer consequence for one's sins. It just seemed to produce an overall entangled sense of strife exampled in the scripture above that seems set opposite the cycle of blessing being described in this book about the power of blessing.

How I would have longed to be blessed within a week by a miraculous reward for praying a blessing over someone who opposed me. It just wasn't the case. The journey has taught me a lot. I hope the naïve purity I once knew could be one day embodied in the wisdom I've since suffered. Jesus instructed his disciples to venture out in their evangelical call remembering always his warning: *Be wise as a serpent and harmless as a dove.*

It's easier to be harmless in the ignorant innocence of childhood. Unfortunately, the transition to adult responsibilities demands a far greater understanding of the robbery the world endures and "children" of all ages, and even the innocent, perpetrate. There are few so innocent and pure as children by adulthood, yet all must effort to mature in the muck of life in some fashion along the way. The scripture calls the heart deceitfully wicked despite declaring men are made in the image of God.

Recently, I tried to clean my kitchen table with the only rag I had, and it was not fresh. I ended up pushing the grime around uselessly. I suddenly remembered another verse in the Old Testament stating that all our good works are as filthy rags next to God's holiness. Another psalm states the Lord looked for a righteous man in all the earth and found none; *no, not one.* So, no one comes out absolutely pure in the end. This neither robs the righteous one of his honor, nor does it dishonor a holy God. Yet, it is a truth to be honored in itself.

If I am unavoidably dirty and tainted from sin, even simple sin born of ignorance and not evil, how is it that I experienced once upon a time a sense of divinity wholly separated from any error or wickedness—in the new age practices I stumbled upon in my mid-twenties? In this one season of life, my senses and ability to perceive powerful spiritual realities were starkly set on fire. I "burned bright" for some reason I never came to know or understand. I knew beyond doubt that: *I am greater than my ability to comprehend my true reality and being. Only heaven knows this truth. I am left to search it out.*

That said, in all my limits expanding, I began to experience different dimensions of reality completely sober. I naturally pursued what I later discovered were yogic practices of meditation and breathing. I began focusing the power of my consciousness in ways I didn't understand and had no previous inkling I was even capable of wielding such authority of being. I didn't know the gospel then and all the power packed into Faith that it describes. With but a mustard seed of pure faith, one is said to be able to move a mountain. Woah. Naturally, as crazy as that may sound, one is left to consider that pure faith is rare and perhaps costly. So, I imagine now, God granted me to experience my divine power, redeemed in Christ, apart from the knowledge of His salvation reigning over me, unaware of Him.

Despite understanding this now, I still grapple with this remembrance in the present. The times my heart speaks a truth conflicting with the overriding justice I'm enduring, I wonder. When my heart accepts a lie, and I experience God's grief, I wonder. When my heart seems to conflict in it's intuition with the will I sense in the Lord, I wonder. When I witness the souls that seem to find freedom in the peace, dignity, and love of their divine spirit and essence apart from the born-again grace purchased by their Savior, I wonder. I realize the God who introduced me to His saving love in His sacrifice knows and loves and redeems beyond a person's awareness of Him. I have heard salvation rest in so simple a commitment as a statement of faith and surrender on one's death bed.

I believe the prophetic warning in the book of Joel is a call to salvation beyond man's understanding. In this prophecy, the Lord proclaims He will save all who call upon the name of the Lord. I imagine the end times and the suffering and tribulation so many endure even now in earthquakes and tsunamis and all the insane circumstances that would confront a person with the sudden and dire need for a Savior before any missionary gets to them.

So, if I'm sitting in a yoga class, amongst women bowing their heads to the Universe and not praising the King of Kings ruling over it, I'm still jealous of their freedom of spirit. They are free to love, they are free in their divine dignity, they are free to be the best people they can be, simply. They share and celebrate life and aim in their own way to create heaven on earth.

I'm trapped! These women are "Worldly," yet not. I am "Christian," yet not. I want that divinity and simplicity, but I am held to a different account, knowing the Savior as I was shown. I once knew what these women live, too. Later, I was called into a different experience and purpose in my life. I was blessed with the great grace and responsibility of being invited into the fellowship of the Son. This calling and my efforts to find my way forward in the pleasure and blessing of God, brought me to bear witness of His spirit and ways from a sort of periphery of inclusion. This was and is yet painful and confusing, confounding and frustrating.

The women in both these settings—both the Bible study and the yoga class—seem free to exercise an autonomy and authority that I desire and admire. I once knew it and now strive to come into such a life once again. It is a providence and grace I never realized was actually shaped and granted by my Maker. Much as I wish my life was different, all I can accept now is that He is content in His wisdom to allow me to endure what I can't understand just to fight my way to freedom.

It is no given to be one of His. I was spoiled in my ignorance, guarded and guided as His unwitting child. I was spoiled in my salvation, brought to know His love openly and generously. Now, I live to testify of the tremendous grace and blessing it is to be called a Child of God, to be brought out of the dark and into His marvelous light. I can't imagine a greater grace, a greater adoption. Nor can I imagine a greater loss.

HIGHEST GLORY

Gould Farm

I STARTED THIS BOOK a year ago. I never would have imagined then that I would find myself staying at a farm in Massachusetts like I do now. But, here I am, settled in, working in a "healing community" for those coping with trials and mental illness. Day by day, I step out into this postcard landscape of absolute beauty. The farm is nestled in a forest of trees. I'm on the forestry and grounds and kitchen work teams. It's February and we've just begun tapping sugar maple trees to collect sap for maple syrup. Who would think to find themselves learning such an odd skill at my age? I'm forty and finally got around to tapping trees. Go figure. Yet, I'm part of this unique offering they create each year.

There's a morning meeting each day that includes such details as "new faces," "comings and goings," a weather report, a fun fact, a reading, and a song that ends it. We literally share three meals a day together, work and activities. I've never been so immersed in community. The people are kind and welcoming. Whenever one person leaves even for a weekend, an announcement brings well wishes on their departure. The weather has mostly consisted of a blanket of white snow over everything. Yesterday, however, we set a record high of 76 for February 22, 2018. We held the weekly community meeting in the beautiful sunny afternoon outside.

I must admit, initially, my heart reacted with a bit of defensive prejudice being somewhere that doesn't openly acknowledge the Lord, singing John Denver and Beatles songs to kick off the work day and all. However, it was interesting to learn that the roots of the farm were founded on the hope of Christian charity towards those struggling mentally. The idea was to provide a loving place to belong to community and find healing in meaningful work and service. It is the oldest such place in the US and it has served as a model for many others. Considering my struggle with unemployment, this has helped my morale and spirit. Just to have a productively structured day filled with work and wonderful people has been a real blessing.

When I first arrived, I spoke on the phone with the woman who leads our bible study. She said, "I believe you're there as a missionary." She was opposed to my trip, desiring that I stay and refusing to see me as mentally ill. She came to accept my coming on my promise that I was being obedient to the Lord. Like many Christians, myself included, she doesn't believe in identifying with a mental illness. The scriptures state that God gives you love, power, and a sound mind, the very mind of Christ by His spirit in a believer. To believe you're ill is to identify with the devil's efforts to label you as deficient and flawed rather than loved and supplied in the sufficiency of God's grace. St. Paul dealt with cruel messengers tormenting him, but happened to be denied deliverance directly by the Lord, who stated, *My grace is sufficient for you.* The Bible, then, details an accomplished apostle who would, in this day, possibly be diagnosed schizophrenic by a psychiatrist for hearing voices if the nature of his suffering involved demonic torment.

Then again, there are testimonies that speak a different word. I've been watching a good deal of sermons by Bill Johnson from Bethel church in California. He is a strong believer in the miraculous works of the Spirit. He holds healing prayer sessions at the start and finish of his sermons in which many are miraculously healed in the moment. He has described the Lord healing people of bipolar disorder by the work of the Spirit. I've personally known God to acknowledge the propensity towards this type of tendency chemically in the brain, the up and down of it. At a stage of my early twenties, I too experienced the highs and lows of depression and hypomania. They are definite conditions as any altered state of mind I've known by means of drugs would testify. If you know what drugs that make you high are like, you know hypomania is a state of sober imbalance.

So, it's beautiful that God would heal the cause miraculously, and it's wise to be careful with how you identify your being. To identify as mentally ill could come from many motives and serve many purposes. Just as it is sensitive to identify as an alcoholic, it is simply a matter to be handled with care. While I don't personally agree with identifying as mentally ill myself just because my experience is so undoubtedly spiritual to me, I know some take it very seriously, especially due to advocacy.

I once heard angels declare into my spirit, "She's speaking life over you" when a friend was stating that she disagreed with my family's insistence on that I have mental illness and not demons. It's important to speak life and not death. Proverbs 18:21 states, *Death and life are in the power of the tongue, and those who love it will eat its fruits.* So, it's paramount to speak life over your soul and others, and not to curse with your speech for you express agreement with a definition of your very being in doing so.

Now, this statement—that I was sent as a missionary—struck me. That's crazy, I thought, given my struggles with reconciliation. My very hope would be to be restored to a state I would assume a missionary would know, not to be someone as beset with trial and insecurity as I've been. Yet, despite my personal doubts, I have encountered two distinct individuals with whom I had the opportunity to share my faith that I would never have anticipated I would meet. Both young men sought out my insights in what seemed to be personal searches for understanding about life.

With one young man, it started at the lunch table. As we sat conversing, he started to go through a little box of "table topic" conversation starter cards. He settled on one and turned to me, confronting me with, "Have you ever had an encounter with an angel?" Well, I ended up sharing a bit about my experiences, and he shared a mystical experience he'd had, too. He seemed to really take interest in my experience. Then one day, he turned to me and said, "So, when are we going to talk about God?" Well, talk about direct! That caught me off guard. So, I invited him to lunch at the farm bakery café that weekend. Given he'd shared his favorite poem with me, I wrote out a series of scriptures to share at our meal.

I discovered his one passion at this point of his life is to pursue Buddhist meditation. He is even considering life as a monastic. He asked me questions that allowed me to share my views and experiences with God. Yet, we never got around to discussing the verses I'd written out. We have met several weekends since then, discussing all manners of topics and issues in life. We've gotten to know each other as friends.

There is an "appreciations" time in our weekly community meeting. This last week, he raised his hand and publicly declared how much he's valued our conversations. I was shocked. So, I raised my hand, suddenly aware I had that to be thankful for as well, but also failed to thank him for helping me to edit and proofread my seminary application essays. He's been ministering to me about my application efforts and all my anxiety about possible rejection and what will I do instead and so on.

His manner is absolutely genteel. A true gentleman, wise and gifted, of all things, in poetry. He can recite a lengthy poem with utterly accurate soul from memory as though rifling through a file drawer of possible poems to choose from—truly uncanny, and genius actually. So, he's been the voice of reason and insight to me for this time. When he offered to edit, I knew this was a blessing, especially given his gift for writing.

But, it never occurred to me to thank him during "appreciations." So, I raised my hand and declared that I, too, valued our conversations and was especially grateful that he'd helped me with my essays. Most everyone in my life here knew I was eagerly awaiting an answer about my acceptance. What they didn't know was that I'd gotten the congratulatory email that morning. I kept it quiet from the meeting, but afterward, since I was sitting right next to my friend, I shared my news with him.

His reaction shocked me and him. He was taken aback with happiness for me and my news. I was so touched and surprised. Proverbs 27:19 states, *Just as water reflects the face, so one human heart reflects another.* For as deeply as he obviously cared for my fate, I was amazed at the friend I'd found here in this time.

Evangelical Efforts

S O, WHILE MY friend and I have yet to talk about the scriptures I wrote out, we've come to share a sweet caring and space in our friendship. I've wondered what God's path is for his soul. He is clearly passionate about meditation and Buddhism in a way that reveals a sense of calling to me. And yet, I wonder, as I read and watch preachers that insist salvation is paramount. I, myself, feel this way, especially given my struggles and experiences.

I was pointed to Romans chapter 3 today, as well. Verses 21-25 state, *But now, apart from law, the righteousness of God has been disclosed, and is attested by the law and the prophets, the righteousness of God through faith in Jesus Christ for all who believe. For there is no distinction, since all have sinned and fall short of the glory of God; they are now justified by his grace as a gift, through the redemption that is in Christ Jesus, whom God put forward as a sacrifice of atonement by his blood, effective through faith.*

This means salvation by faith matters to each soul; and yet, in my own experience, I know that God is the one in charge of a soul's salvation. In the gospel of John, Jesus told his disciples, *You did not choose me but I chose you. John 15:16* So, I am but a messenger or intermediary. Perhaps even an intercessor, but no more.

One Sunday at church, shortly after I got saved, I saw this one beautiful girl I knew holding the communion plate. When I walked up to her to take a piece of bread, she looked so delighted to see me, sweetly surprised. She said, "You're here!" I said, "Yes, the Lord saved me." We hadn't seen each other for years. We used to study together in grad school. She said, "I prayed for your salvation back then and hoped in this." I was touched. The thought that this sweet soul had been praying for me was so amazing and generous and gracious to me.

Now, I've been the one to hope on another's salvation and to watch and wait, watch and wait. Yet, there are those who "lead people to the Lord" and simply share the gospel and pray the sinner's prayer with someone who gets saved right then and there—talk about amazing! Nevertheless, it took years for this girl's silent prayers to come to pass.

I realize God stepped into my life in a particular moment by His own miraculous will and not by any evangelist ministering to me. Then again, I once heard a spirit-filled woman pray over me: "The Father and the Son have come after you so many times..." and I knew she was likely referring to at least some of the evangelists that tried to reach out to me over the years. Had I been more open in my mind and heart and come to accept Christ in faith sooner, I sure would have lived a better life and saved myself a great deal of heartache from sin I didn't take seriously enough. Yet, I have sinned even against grace in my personality and the pressures I faced.

So, there's just no telling what God's will is with regard to any particular individual's salvation. Salvation is the beginning of an open fellowship with one's Maker, and this is no small affair. There needs to be a preparedness in the timing of such a beginning in one's life. So, in the case of my friend's life, I'm holding our conversations open handedly. I also want to learn about his passion. It clearly means a lot to him and so that means I have something to learn in love.

I'm hoping that loving in this way will honor the Lord's lessons to me about love. I valued scripture and seeking wisdom over personal responsibility and love of my family at points. I let my hunger and zeal get into the way of the true priority at the time. I feel like I'm letting the priority lead me this time. I also just like the care we share, just as it is.

Jesus spoke quite highly of friendship. In the gospel of John, He said, *"This is my commandment, that you love one another as I have loved you. No one has greater love than this, to lay down one's life for one's friends. You are my friends if you do what I command you. I do not call you servants any longer, because the servant does not know what the master is doing; but I have called you friends, because I have made known to you everything I have heard from my Father... I am giving you these commands so that you may love one another." John 15:12-17* So, I am content to love my friend just as he is. And I feel the Lord's pleasure in our friendship.

To feel the Lord's pleasure is one thing, deeply assuring and gratifying as it may be. It is entirely another thing to feel other emotions that I know belong to Him and not to me, distinctly. Then, add to this strange reality and blessing the experience of His heart for someone else. I had a friend once who shared something I'll never forget as we conversed one night. As she ministered to me, she became uncomfortable. She confessed she felt suddenly overwhelmed with a distinct love for me, her friend, that was significantly deeper than her love for her own children. She knew it was Him and testified faithfully despite feeling disturbed.

I believe her because I've known some intense emotions of love for another that did not belong to me at all. This is what happened with the other young man I met. He started the program just before I arrived. We shared this in common and got along easily. One night, we ended up in a deeper conversation about life. At some point, he shared about an incident that was clearly traumatic and troubling. Well, this event apparently was deeply wrong and drew out this instant flash of powerful anger in me, a fiercely protective love towards this young man. The Lord was not happy about this event, to say the least. And here I was, privy to his heart about this injustice I knew nothing of; but, this much I knew—God *loves* this young man.

I started to think of him. I felt a care in me towards his well being. While this was not the Lord's emotion, He did give me a heart of love for him. I realized after some time that he was searching spiritually. He confessed feeling drawn to Christianity. After some deliberation, I decided to indulge my desire to buy him a book I was reading, <u>A Purpose Driven Life</u> by Rick Warren. It is essentially an introduction and guide to faith in Christ for someone unaware of this knowledge. I confided about my experience of the Lord's love for him. He asked to learn more, confessing his ignorance of who Jesus was and what faith in Him means. We met and talked. I was touched by his gentle search and questions of my experiences and trials. I had another blessed chance to share, much as I hope this book can save another some of my struggles.

One Day at a Time

SINCE GETTING NEWS of acceptance into seminary this last week, I've prepared my return flight to start school in a little over a month. I have mixed feelings about this farm. On the one hand, I am eager to get home to my cat and effort to find a job and my community of friends from back home. On the other, I am only just beginning to develop a deeper heart for this new group of people I've known now for the last couple of months. I am relieved to stay longer than I anticipated initially, having heard from the Lord that I was to stay for two months. Now, it is more like three months. I know I'm getting attached, and I like it, but also fear it. It will be hard to say goodbye soon enough now.

My mom asked me recently, "How is your progress honey?" I was caught off guard. Progress? I suddenly felt like a cake baking in the oven. Is she cooked through yet? I'm almost done, Mom. I had no idea what to say, so I was honest. "I don't really know what to say Mom. I don't feel like I'm making progress I guess. I'm just living." I hope she wont be disappointed by whatever she is hoping this stay will achieve. I'm just taking the next step of faith, being the same person I've ever been. I'm still hoping for deliverance and that's going to be progress when it comes—years of the same struggle come to an end is what that would be.

When I was yet putting my application together, and I felt discouraged, the Lord impressed on my heart—*Have faith*. I realized then that I was indulging anxiety. Still, it felt like prudent realism at the time. How do you have faith exactly? Well, at each turn that I wondered if things would work out, they did. The recommendation letters came in time. The transcripts arrived in time. Everything came together by the deadline, unlike all my anxiety. Then, I became convinced I would never be accepted once I submit the application. One night, laying in bed, I brainstormed five different alternative life paths I could pursue. I could try other Bible colleges. I could try a master's of social work. I could try public health. And on and on.

The day before I got the email, as I reflected in my discouragement, I heard—*perhaps the Lord will grant it as a generosity.* And so it was. Even yet, as I reflected on this just last night, awoken from sleep, I was informed this wasn't a fair assessment to share publicly. Apparently, I've earned this grace in so far as the Lord's been pleased in my devotion to "matters of the heart."

He reminded me of a proverb I was studying recently. Proverbs 21:2 states, *All deeds are right in the sight of the doer, but the LORD weighs the heart.* I was surprised. Sure, I try to do right, but what good news to hear that the Lord is actually pleased in my heart's posture in my deeds. He told me He was pleased in my devotion to scripture, my commitment to speaking up about abortion, my pursuit of journalism about the foster care system, and my ministry towards other souls.

Perhaps there is hope. Although I still yet await deliverance, I will be pursuing a Master of Divinity after all. This was step one to that vision of a dream I was granted some months ago now. I should be excited and I am most definitely relieved and eagerly anticipating class, but I am facing the unfolding of that dream in the reality of its first step and it's just real, not a plan on a page. That's still sinking in.

What does it mean to become a minister? This question now confronts me, and I realize I have no idea, nor do I have the excitement and confidence I knew heading into my studies at CFNI once upon a time. At that time, I was pure zeal, with zero concern for what such a question bears. I just loved God with all of myself (that I knew of anyway) and the rest was irrelevant. I believe that is how it ought to be. I find it unfortunate to be as I am now. For all the trial and difficulty that's tempered that zeal with disappointment, I can't say I'm zealous anymore.

On the other hand, I've developed a definite and deeper respect for the realities of faith in Christ. I can say I've praised God from the pits of my being, more selflessly than I've yet known. I can say that obedience is paramount, even to zeal, as a demonstration of love in respect for God's authority. That said, I've also known just how much pure love means to the Lord. My former purity of zeal sure did offset a great deal of sins that I believe He was merciful towards on account of this passionate love, gratitude, and praise.

Facing this new blessing though, I know one thing: no matter my condition or circumstance, I sure hope I fulfill this opportunity with my best potential. I am grateful for the chance to serve. This open door also gives me the beginning of faith in my future. I am just barely able to trust that Jeremiah 29:11 actually applies to me and my future is bright despite all my shortcomings, failures, and sins against grace. I'm just beginning to trust in the hope of a blessed destiny granted. One day, perhaps, I can look back on that destiny, that vision of a dream, and say, faith won and mercy triumphed in my life, praise be to God!

My sister sent me a necklace recently. It was titled "One Day at a Time." The little plaque that came with it states, *One day at a time—this is enough. Don't be in such a rush to figure everything out. Be patient with yourself and your journey. Breathe and concentrate where you are today. You may not be where you want, but you are exactly where you need to be. Trust the process and remember that you get to your destination when the timing is right. It may not feel like it, but forward is forward, no matter if it is one moment at a time, one step at a time, or one day at a time. So, let life surprise you, embrace the unknown, and remember that all good things take time.*

I think this is the key to that day down the line that I hope on. Psalm 27:13-14 states, *I believe that I shall see the goodness of the LORD in the land of the living. Wait for the LORD; be strong and let your heart take courage; wait for the LORD!* So, while my future is unfolding to a bit more light, and I still await deliverance, I'll just take it one day at a time. Work one day at a time. Pursue goodness one day at a time. Love the Lord one day at a time. Love others one day at a time. And then, hopefully, one day I'll look back and say...

Faith Going Forward

PSALM 3:8 SAYS, *Deliverance belongs to the LORD; may your blessing be on your people.* To be a delivered child of God is blessing indeed. I've slept in peace for the last three nights. All day today, I've had peace of mind. I'm hoping these are the beginnings of my breakthrough. I thought I had all but finished this book, having already birthed the last chapter in a few nights awoken by the strong urge to write.

I thought my story would end with a ray of light shining into the life of a girl still hoping on deliverance. Well, just like the Lord told me to "have faith" when it came to submitting my application, He's telling me now "have faith" with regard to deliverance and my return to the Woodlands and the start of school. I've always wondered what this statement actually means. What does it look like to "have faith" anyway?

Usually, I confuse prudent realism with anxiety in a mish-mash of striving to address the unknown with my effort and control. Just yesterday I had two distinct experiences arise that shed light on this confusion for me. First, in the morning, I was checking my email and upon seeing a post from my job board, I was tempted to search the updated list of findings for potential job matches. I've already applied to seven jobs. I've been warned, *Don't apply to anymore.* That's hard to obey.

What if none of the seven contact me like the pile of applications that came to nought for the last three years? Surely, applying to more openings increases my chances of getting a job. But, chances and faith are not compatible. Faith says there is a right job, not just any job I'm lucky enough to be blessed with like it would seem humility would speak. Nope. Faith sits tight and waits for the job to come in the right timing by the grace of God.

Well, given the instructions, it's easy enough to resist the urge to continue applying and try to feel out this faith thing. I still didn't get it though. *But Lord, I don't deserve this. You mean just apply to a handful and wait? I should be working daily.* Why would it be that easy? I don't trust things that don't take enough work, effort, odds that are ultimately against "humble" me, lucky to get one in a hay stack, so demoralized I am after these years of unemployment.

Yet, as I was faced with this email, testing and tempting me again, I felt this sudden awareness come over me. It's as though life and the Lord somehow put it to my heart and mind and soul—TRUST and WAIT. I was able to actually experience what it felt like. I tasted this faith and boy was it sweet, brief as it may have been passing through me. If "it" could speak, this state of soul would say, "Sit back and watch God bless you in His generosity. He is able and working on your behalf. Just thank Him and wait in patient gratitude. And enjoy the wait, praising the King in advance for your victory." Woah. Oh my!

So, that's the antithesis of anxiety. By evening I was walking to dinner, and I was suddenly hit with the reflection, *Anxiety really is a sin after all!* I always found it a bit messed up that anxiety and unbelief were counted as sin in the scriptures. Psalm 37:8 says, *Do not fret—it leads only to evil.* For heavens sake, it's torturous enough to endure fretting as it is, much less to be sinning as you're trying your best to cope anyway, being a puny human and all. Well, apparently trusting in God's sovereign power and good, gracious character is the true way to honor Him. When I think it's all on me, I'm essentially presuming to be entirely responsible and considering I'm not and there only so much I control, I end up anxious and striving.

It's not been lost on me that I end up "getting in the way" sometimes, never mind wasting time duplicating needless effort in the name of prudence and "hard work," self-satisfied, but hardly demonstrating honor towards God in trust. I guess I could apply all that unnecessary time, effort, and attention more usefully in reality if I was actually seeking His spirit and will instead. What would He have me do with all the time I spend striving in my own strength? I have no idea honestly. This is all quite the epiphany in reality even if I've heard it and already considered it conceptually for so long. I'm going to have to try all this out and see what happens.

Hebrews 11:1-3 states, *Now faith is the assurance of things hoped for, the conviction of things not seen... By faith we understand that the worlds were prepared by the word of God, so that what is seen was made from things that are not visible.* So, technically, I hope for a job. It is currently nonexistent, at least to my sight. What legitimate assurance can I look to in order that I should continue to wait in faith for what I fear may never arrive? Well, I have the experience granted about waiting for one's victory while thanking and praising the Lord. That was after a bad encounter with my mom, too. Sin can stand in the way of a promise fulfilled sometimes.

Proverbs 10:28 says, *The hope of the righteous ends in gladness, but the expectation of the wicked comes to nothing.* Therefore, these promises are contingent upon one's righteous standing in the Lord. All I can think is that I repented and apologized to my mom and then rebuked myself privately with a teaching on how I could handle it rightly in the future. Incidentally, my fall came in reacting in anger towards offense against me. My pride responded. If I had kept my calm, prayed quietly, and continued to love past the offense, then I would have fulfilled my Christian expectation and potential. I would have blessed mercy and love over strife.

Proverbs 10:6 states, *Blessings are on the head of the righteous, but the mouth of the wicked conceals violence.* Well, my mom hasn't accepted my schooling dreams yet. She's concerned they aren't practical and wont support me financially after incurring a great deal of debt. These are absolutely natural concerns given the pursuit of a three year Master's degree at a private school. And yet, I've come this far on faith and am trusting my way forward. However, at one point in our call, the words, "Well, you still need to fix yourself" pierced me. I've always felt insufficient in light of my Mom's expectations. I'm messed up, lesser than she hopes for me.

There's a part of me well aware I'm short of my own desires for self and there's natural legitimacy to her concerns. Yet, my humanity wants to say: *back off, I'm always trying to fix myself for the better, Mom.* Proverbs 10:12 says, *Hatred stirs up strife, but love covers all offenses.* So, the ticket to my righteous standing is to LOVE through every possible offense with pure, gentle, merciful compassion, as best I can muster in my fallen humanity. My job is to be faithful and love no matter. No matter what? Just no matter. Yup. So, there's one stickler. Love is a lot of things. Like, being nice, being forgiving, being understanding, being encouraging, believing and having faith in your friend, being reliable, being devoted and loyal, being...obedient?

To Jesus, loving is obedience. It is perhaps all those other things, too. But specifically, He told his disciples in John 15:12-17, *This is my commandment, that you love one another as I have loved you. No one has greater love than this, to lay down one's life for one's friends. You are my friends if you do what I command you...* So, to obey is to love and to love is to obey. For example, I obeyed to stop applying to jobs despite the urgency or anxiety to keep at it. Now, this call of obedience to God's spirit is in conflict with my mother. Honor thy parents and it will go well with you. To obey my mother's wish is to stay at this farm another few months and postpone the first term of school. Is this to love my mother? Was it not the Lord that confirmed my spring application and then my admission?

Furthermore, my counselor, sister, and father all agree—stay longer. It's just me and my invisible God (and, mind you, I'm the "mentally ill" one), so if God doesn't prove me true, I'm just hearing things or confused in my thinking or I just made a stubborn, poor choice in the face of overwhelming counsel. The fact that I never asked for the promise of a car, job, or deliverance seems odd. I figured this book would end without deliverance, but with the hope of school. Then, a promise was granted— *watch and see, He's going to vindicate you when you get back to the Woodlands.*

In this vindication, I was supposed to receive a car by means that were not my parents. I was supposed to receive a job relevant to my work and training history. I was supposed to be delivered from all the demonic torment I've suffered. I even got an interesting taste of this the other night. I spoke with my academic advisor, Jeremiah, for about an hour. He said he felt led to recommend I take a class called "Pastoral Ministry." I got chills when he said that.

I felt the Lord nudging me, saying essentially, *You didn't know I've got a different purpose in mind than what you imagined.* Being a pastor? Never in my wildest dreams would I ever fathom such a calling. Well, by the end of our conversation, he asked to pray for me. I accepted. Just as we were going to say goodbye, he said, "Wait a minute, the Holy Spirit's telling me to ask you to pray for me." I was shocked. I rarely pray at all. Yes, an oddity perhaps considering everything. I just feel so defiled by darkness that I generally don't feel worthy to pray.

So, I felt shocked and grateful the Lord would ask me directly. Wow! So, I accepted and asked Jeremiah what was going on in his life. He opened up and shared with me. I felt so honored to learn about him and his personal struggle for faith. I sensed a natural prayer rise up in me. It felt so good to pray for him! After we hung up, I went to the dining hall for dinner in a haze. I felt like I was walking on a cloud. As I sat to eat my dinner, I felt such a deep sense of dignity and worth. I had no strange anxiety about eating. I ate like I imagine so many "normal" people must feel when they eat. I was overwhelmed with this abiding sense of prophesy that said, "You are inherently loved by heaven and will come to serve the Lord in a great purpose." Now, I hear in my spirit the word, "destiny."

This wouldn't just be "deliverance." This was so much more. Here I was, confronted by school starting, confronted by a calling I'd never imagined, and confronted by the bold decision to leave the farm, my home of over two months at that point. It would seem like an easy decision to leave and start school. However, I faced literally every caring soul in my life warning me with all their hearts, *Stay until the summer and postpone school.*

Biblically, it's wisdom to heed trustworthy counsel in your life—not to make rebellious decisions that don't do justice to those who truly care for you. Then, it is also wisdom to heed the counsel of the authorities placed in your life. Both my parents and my counselor agreed I should stay. Then there's the fact that I knew God was using my family as His instruments through the last 6 months of my life, my sister especially. I could see Him using her heart and intuition to guide me forward in His will. So, I've learned enough in spiritual wisdom and discernment to realize the importance of heeding counsel.

Basically, I was left with His will that two months prior had pointed me to apply to the Spring term versus all this counsel. I felt a personal ambition to not postpone a three year degree any longer, burdened by the sense that I'm already too old and so on—all these insecurities about life that really don't amount to anything necessarily. One could argue it's equally important to get solid footing before started such an undertaking, which was probably at the heart of their reasoning anyway.

Nevertheless, eager to get started and also to experience the promises that were spoken over my return, I denied the overwhelming counsel and chose to stand instead on my Lord's Word to me. Incidentally, He eventually confessed to me this choice expressed pleasing faith to Him, which shocked me! I learned still a little more about this thing called faith.

The Woodlands

THE "FAVOR" OF the Lord is not something one considers when your highest hope of years is deliverance and restoration. However, I got a slight taste of this coming back to the Woodlands, and it's such a beautiful reality in faith that it's worth a short description for those who are perhaps learning. I will say, I used to know a life of greater favor prior to losing my salvation, and oddly, even prior to getting saved. I can say the Lord most definitely covered me in love and grace that made me even wonder why my life seemed to bless me so richly well before I ever knew of Him or believed.

That said, favor is a spiritual condition in which God is gazing upon you and your life with love and pleasure, shining the light of His blessings on all your circumstances. For example, you may get multiple job offers, all vying to be chosen. That house deal you've been waiting on comes through with money in your pocket—a steal of a deal worked out in loving kindness between two willing parties, both mutually blessed. Now, because *that* worked out in just the *exact way* that it did, the dream you've held out for saving up, just got the perfect lift. Perhaps, when the right steps align, and you *feel* they are, even the dream will come to pass to the praise and the pleasure of the King. Because, you believe in all His goodness and love, He is arranging your circumstances for your best blessing even as you wait for it all to line up.

When I first arrived, I was mired in dark dreams and the same demonic presences. Nevertheless, a good bit of hope yet drove me forward in a fresh zeal, in part because being accepted to seminary in the grace of the Lord was a tremendous affirmation of my faith and standing in the Lord. On this hope, I embraced all the tasks I set for myself to accomplish. I finished a short documentary I made about the farm that I was able to share with my new friends up north and my community in the Woodlands. I applied to nanny jobs. Indeed, this one day, with a strong sense of faith abiding in me, I received a request from an interested family. I sensed I was to be with them from our first phone call. They hired me at our first meeting.

I knew the job was a gift from the Lord because, aside from sensing it, the family were kind, down-to-earth Christians who didn't require that I have my own car. This was an absolute rarity in the countless job offers I applied to. Just about everyone required applicants to provide their own car. So, not only was this an unusual blessing, but they also happened to live about a mile and a half away, a mere bike ride. I invested in a bike and got started part time. The schedule nicely complemented my classes and other duties. I realized this was the perfect fit for my life and thought back on the faith experience I had. Plus, we got along great over time and they became people I truly cared for who have blessed me so much. This was one sign of favor heartening me upon my return.

Soon enough, I invested in a used car that turned out to be a real steal for it's quality. Again the man was a Christian and the Lord told me not to even bargain the price down. It was already priced nicely in my favor. Thus, I began the scary journey of adapting to the roads again after a five year hiatus. I have since become a typical road warrior and actually crave driving. I enjoy it so much now. Such a chance to wield perfect control and authority when life otherwise may lack it.

Class was a major shift of consciousness. I was slowly and cautiously adapting to the possibility of becoming a pastor someday. This was nothing I could have come up with. This was purely the Lord's idea. As much as I felt surprised and insecure, I also came to rest in this tremendous sense of purpose and calling as though nestling into a much needed pillow or cushion. For all the insanity I had ever endured pursuing Him and His Word, I drank up my new purpose in faith. Nonetheless, shocked, I held this new gift gently.

Slowly, I considered I might actually enjoy being a pastor just because I have some of the abilities and strengths that seem to fit their work. I love to talk to people and got over any fears of public speaking starting with high school debate long ago. I love doing research and studying the Bible.

I love doing projects as a team. So, even though I didn't come up with it, I was certainly feeling privileged to imagine and work towards it.

As the quarter terms went on, I found myself pleading with the Lord—*please help me!* The mental cruelty was tough to bear. He tried to console me to be patient and endure. He told me He would deliver me when the time was right. He wanted me to press against all the evils I was enduring with my best effort at righteousness. It made sense to me, but I tell you, I hardly felt like any kind of spiritual warrior. I was stewed in a diet of doubt, mockery, bullying, and general cruelty. Much of it mocked my calling and efforts at deliverance. *You're just a wannabe chasing after no King that wants me. Like you'd ever be a pastor anyway, "faster"* (since I'm always fasting). *Keep trying loser. He'll deliver you someday, surely He will.* And so on.

Eventually, I struggled hard to feel a sense of security and sanction in my calling and in going to school. It grew steeper and steeper—the bank of my climb to freedom and deliverance. The more I struggled, the more I stumbled clinging to comforts and crutches (sin), the more I suffered consequences, the less ground was actually supporting my standing in the Lord.

He's supposed to be the Rock on which you found your home, the refuge and shelter covering you in the storm. All the benefits of faith in Him depend on your obedience and holiness. Sin takes away the cover and the ground turns to sand. Much as I pursued righteousness each day, I also struggled with sin, mostly eating emotionally or expressing disrespect in my frustration with God.

I often felt demoralized, yet I would receive grace in the face of being emptied to the dregs of my soul's strength to fight. For example, this one time, I awoke in the morning from a difficult night of dark dreams and knew I had received the grace of "strength" in the Lord—I've grown to discern the feeling of this in my body. He expected me to exert that strength, even faced with my state of mind. All I wanted was to curl up into a ball and retreat to a dark, silent space to be alone and heal. But, indeed, my Sergeant wanted His ever-loving Marine to get up and go running.

It wasn't such a dire request. It's not like I had to go on a search and rescue in the cold, black night waters of the ocean. Just go running. But, I felt so justified... *I must heal, Lord!* This was not pleasing for His will in my development. I thought He was Insane. What sort of human does

He expect me to be? A Cross-Carrying Human. Literally. I just wanted to say, but I'm not You. I'm not cut out for this. But no, He insisted, *You don't know your limits or your potential. I. Do. And your not pushing yourself sufficiently in my sight. I expect more self sacrifice from you.*

Much as that felt like some sort of compliment, I grew tired of falling short of such demands. Unbeknownst to me, my Lord grew tired of my ingratitude for His loving presence. I was taking Him for granted, and His patience was wearing thin. I was so used to His presence. I even presumed it was an alm for my suffering, to help me to survive the torment. I honestly began hosting self-pity and self-righteousness like the beginning of mold in a damp environment. Unaware I was hosting such risky character traits, trying my hardest daily to be my best, I was the perfect candidate for the fall I was about to take that would cost me so much. As ingratitude goes, you don't know what you've got until you lose it.

My Fall

EVENTUALLY, I GREW more disillusioned I'd ever satisfy my God's will for my righteous fight. I felt He was cruel and unfair. By the next turn, I'd defend Him. He's justified, I reasoned. I should be so blessed He'd even expect that much from me, that He'd work with me so diligently to develop my discipline and righteousness in the first place. I had two ends of my being. I loved Him, and I'd grown to resent Him. The sense of ruin felt so powerful one night, I asked Him, "How can Love come from this? I don't see any hope of future love. And if not, then please, just leave me." Now, I've begged through thick and thin for years and years: *Please don't leave, please don't leave.* He's been faithful to me for so long. Little did I realize how offensive my faithlessness was this night.

I came to understand in a dream that He was upset with me for my faithless ingratitude. It's as though your friend is standing loyally by your side and just because there's a war happening, you declare to him, "There's no hope for us! Just let me be." Well, the friend's possibly feeling like, *Hello, what am I? Am I just loving you day in, day out for nothing? What sort of hope are looking for? Am I not sufficient?* And there are so many songs declaring "You are sufficient!" to praise and adore Him.

The whole sin of idolatry is basically just dissatisfaction—God's not worthy of my devotion, I want God *And* XYZ. I want God *And* Alcohol. I want God *And* Comfort Food. And so on. Or, even worse, I want XYZ so bad, it actually supersedes my desire and honor towards God. Well, my faithless hopelessness competed with God's faithfulness to stay with me all that time. It was a cowardly insult against Him. It was even crowding Him out of my life, giving up in resignation.

If you remember the story of the twelve spies sent to scope out Canaan, God was displeased in the ten faithless spies who insisted the Canaanites were too big to conquer. Only two spies pleased Him, Joshua and Caleb. They came back with a "good report" confident in God's hand on their people and grateful for the rich inheritance the land proved to be in their sight. This was, after all, the land of milk and honey. They found clusters of grapes so huge they had to be carried by two men, hanging from a bar balanced between them.

After the tremendous journey of the Exodus, the Lord was finally ready to share this great gift with the people He miraculously delivered from the bondage of Egyptian slavery. It was a difficult journey that not every former slave was counted worthy to endure. Coming into the promise meant everything. Now, imagine denying the gift in cowardice, unwilling to fight for it. So, of all the spies, Joshua was chosen to lead the charge into Canaan and the Israelites went on to conquer the land just as God had commanded. He declared their victory because He was *with them.* He went into the battle with them. As they say, the battle belongs to the Lord.

Anyway, idolatry is a subject all its own. For now, I just want to say how little I was able to appreciate my sin at the time. I didn't honor the fact that the Lord *was with me.* The battle belonged to Him. I could rest my fears in this fact, and praise Him for His faithfulness to abide with me. I did the opposite, swayed by the sense of certainty in my perception of reality. Like, *are you kidding me?! Have you noticed the Canaanites happen to average 7 feet in height?! You want me to conquer who? The Devil and Anti-christ? Your worst enemy in the earth? Perpetrating the most heinous of evils?* Well, I lost faith in my ability and in Him.

Nevertheless, I felt Right, clear as day. I was totally shocked He got upset. If anything, I figured I was owed some comfort and assurance, some hope in the face of ruin, if there was any. So, strangely, I actually felt royally affirmed by the rebuke. Wow, there is hope after all—I was actually wrong! In all my limited humanity, I couldn't appreciate true hopelessness until a few weeks later when I actually got to taste it.

It's a stark and Insane reality. For just a fleeting moment as I slept one night, I felt absolutely helpless and hopeless, calm yet terrified. I knew I had no control over my soul and where I could end up. I knew I would go to hell with no ability to plead or pray. Time was up. I was no longer my own. And, worst of all was the knowing that this would be *forever*. Now, *that's* hopeless.

There's an interesting scripture in the book of Solomon's wisdom, Ecclesiastes, that states: *Whoso keepeth the commandment shall feel no evil thing: and a wise man's heart discerneth both time and judgment. Because to every purpose there is time and judgment, therefore the misery of man is great upon him. For he knoweth not that which shall be: for who can tell him when it shall be? There is no man that hath power of the spirit to retain the spirit... Ecc 8:5-8 (KJV)*

Psalm 88 is a "Prayer for Help in Despondency" that describes perfectly this midnight reality I endured: *O LORD, God of my salvation, when, at night, I cry out in your presence, let my prayer come before you; incline your ear to my cry. For my soul is full of troubles, and my life draws near to Sheol. I am counted among those who go down to the Pit; I am like those who have no help, like those forsaken among the dead...You have put me in the depths of the Pit, in the regions dark and deep. Your wrath lies heavy upon me, and you overwhelm me with all of your waves.*

Once I knew Hopelessness, I realized retrospectively about that night of my complaint: I had been swimming in *oceans* of hope. I was better able to appreciate my faithlessness. Apparently my humanity and life experience had its limits. I was too wowed by the darkness and too impressed by the ruin. One night, I even thought to myself, better that I would never have known the love of God than to have known its ruin to this measure. This disappointed the Lord. I wasn't appreciating what a tremendous grace it was to know His love.

I felt innocent. It's exactly because that love meant so much to me that I even felt that way. Again, too wowed by ruin and damage. I often thought of marriages or relationships seemingly beyond repair. I guess I don't have God's vantage by any stretch. He is a worker of redemption from situations that appear absolutely hopeless. Heaven knows I've been obsessed with such stories and testimonies.

All this taking-the-Lord-for-granted prompted a spiritual test of my fidelity. For years I had begged the Lord that I be granted the right to "marry" Him. I got rejected several times but kept hoping. He often warned me He may want to bless me with a family. I was never called to be a nun, for heaven's sake. Nevertheless, I'm 41 now and single yet, having made no effort to date, content in my relationship with God. Well, this year I started to feel self conscious. I'm only getting older, and I'm still hoping to "marry" my Lord. Of course, my idea of this marriage involves an overcoming deliverance and restoration to the love I knew in my original salvation. This has been my entire struggle of these years. It's challenged me to the point that I wonder if it's possible at all.

So by the time I got back from the farm, I considered, perhaps I'm being unrealistic and lazy about finding a companion. Someday surely, I'll fail the spiritual hope of overcoming into some salvation love I once knew years ago, and I'll be left old and alone. The burden of realism and mature responsibility for myself was upon me. I thought, I can't look back in five years frustrated with Him, trying to find a companion. So, I half-heartedly got on a dating site.

After a few months with no realistic interactions, I suddenly got a message from someone who seemed like a potential fit. He was close to my age, living in my city, a social worker, and he seemed kind. We exchanged messages and when it came to chatting on the phone, I got warnings: *Don't do this. You'll regret it something fierce. You're going to give away everything that's mattered to you.* You don't get blessed in life with any starker warnings from angels. Even the Lord said to me: *Be a woman of courage and integrity.*

While I trusted and believed these warnings, I literally couldn't see how they were true of my circumstance. I felt justified and innocent in my reasoning and sense of things. In reality, I had to accept my choice was wrong without the luxury of understanding—just like a child trusting in a Father who simply knows what is best and wants it for you. So, for heavens sake, literally, how hard was it to just cut off contact with this man? Easiest decision ever. Yet, in my arrogant rebellion, I insisted on my "right" to a call and even a meeting. I saw this stupid decision through despite every diligent warning on the way.

The call seemed casual to me, as I had defended—innocent. I'm not sinning. In reality, I was directly disobeying the same God who I try day in day out to please, who I've pursued diligently to the very ends of my being, whose Word and Scriptures I've searched my own salvation and righteousness out of for years, *years.* All that time, I'd never sinned quite like this. I literally crowned myself Eve and insisted—"But, this fruit doesn't have anything wrong with it, and it will make me wise."

I insisted on my need to experience one date. I vowed not to pursue any relationship but to fulfill my promise to meet him for dinner. Bottom line, I was testing my own heart. The desired meeting would "make me wise,"—give me experiential understanding of the confusion in me that signed up for the site to begin with months ago. Nevertheless, God essentially warned me: If you eat of this fruit, you will die—spiritually. I ignored the warning blatantly. Sure enough, I "died"—suffering costly consequences that would test the limits of my character.

Always Heed Your Angels

O N MY WAY to meet this guy, I felt an overt, powerful sense of adultery in my heart. I knew I was cheating on the Lord. I knew I was selling out my own heart of love for Him. I presumed His forgiveness of me, this innocent woman needing to just experience herself in this particular way. As I sat through dinner with this man, I distinctly realized, again in my heart, that I had zero desire to ever date another man again. Now that's a done and done heart. I didn't really know that about myself.

Guess who did? God and His angels. They seriously know things in such a strange way that it blows my mind, how intimately known I can be beyond my own self understanding. This instance is nothing compared to other times I've been amazed at the wisdom of heaven. The Bible says in the first letter to the Corinthian church, *For now we see in a mirror, dimly, but then we will see face to face. Now I know only in part; then I will know fully, even as I have been fully known. 1 Cor 13:12*

Nevertheless, I failed to trust the angels' testimony about myself! Realizing I didn't want to date again—I honestly believe that was the knowledge I was seeking. I think I was testing my heart against the encounter. I discovered my truth, but by then, I'd traded my integrity in against every warning for a cheap chance to taste this night as not-a-nun. Why do that? I guess hind sight is 20/20. I imagine how I could have allowed my integrity to declare a complete commitment to my Lord. How good that path tastes to me though it be impossible to take now.

Regret can't undo sin. What if I've lost His commitment forever now, distrusting the depth of my desire? Have I unwittingly forsaken a total heart in the face of insight? In retrospect, the warnings not only made sense to me, but struck me for their absolute accuracy. I guess this is a lesson as much about the very Word of God as any angelic declaration. His scriptures are guidance to man from a Heavenly Father.

In reality, this test was about many things, some unrelated to any devotion or adultery. Commitment to God encompasses the entirety of life. Part of my argument for meeting with this man was that perhaps the spiritual battle I'd patiently born up with little seeming success wasn't something I'd ever overcome. Perhaps I just wasn't cut out for marrying a holy King. I was justifying resignation, imagining a way out of "the battle." I was giving up for a better hope, as if I could escape my trial anyway. There was no other option truly.

Nevertheless, I considered: *Isn't there value and dignity to the life of so many I see that aren't chasing after a holy King against the Devil?* Yes, I was a zealous convert once upon a time, blessed should I ever know the chance to martyr myself like those in the Bible whom I admired. Undying love for a God every bit worthy of every ounce of one's being. Living a life of devoted and true love was my dream of years; however, this became less and less real in the face of my unfolding humanity struggling to merely redeem the twists and turns of my life.

Prior to going on the date, I tried reasoning with my patient Lord. I pointed out that the Spirit-filled reverend woman I met years ago living out of her van in her sixties, chasing unrealistically lofty dreams—hers was not my idea of a successful life. I admired the more down-to-earth grit of my own atheist sister, diligently working and raising a family. I argued, though she is not a believer and may not know the glories of being guided by the Holy Spirit of God, she yet knows the blessing of the Father and lives a life of love and honor. I was warned again, *Always reach for and hope in the highest glory.* The reverend woman, no matter how she may seem to me or anyone else, enjoys a life of communion and friendship with her Maker and looks forward to an eternity in His love. This is the glory the Lord died for and to abandon it denies His due, aside from forsaking the true value in one's own life.

None of that made any sense to me, until I suffered the consequences that followed my disobedience. First, I had to make peace with having lost my calling. There is a spirit realm with laws and rights and battles and tests. I "gave it away to Satan" wholesale, in deliberate, direct, disobedient rebellion at that, cheating on my love for God and His faithfulness to abide with me through my trial. I did all this arguing the worthiness of a life outside of God's Kingdom, outside of His glory.

Losing my calling meant I lost my right to continue in school. This disruption of my life and its flow, its assumption, its expectation, of everything that I'd suffered up to that point fighting for, this sudden amputation of purpose left me reeling with arguments. *No, this can't be! This is not fair! You're able to pardon me, surely! You can forgive me, Lord!* And on and on. In the book of Genesis, Jacob's brother Esau also sold out and fought for his lost inheritance, begging his father's blessing with tears. But, it was too late.

I got flatly denied. *No, you had warnings. No, you're no child anymore. No, I've already saved you many times. No, you must face the consequence.* Much as I couldn't argue any of this, I grew more and more desperate. I started accusing the King: *You promised me this and that, You're not fair or true,* etc. I spoke with increasing audacity, insisting: *I'm worthy! I never got a true chance! I've had to fight for every inch!* Well, true as that may have been, everything I fought for I gave away in a day, apparently. This decision carried weight I could never have imagined. They did try to warn me.

Just when I should have been repentant, I became increasingly arrogant and irreverent, desperately pleading my case. I should have apologized for failing to obey my Lord's warnings for my own sake. I should have had sorrow for my faithlessness selling out my own heart's love and truth just to taste "the other side." I should have accepted all this cost me steeply and submit to the consequences humbly, hoping on mercy to cover my way forward. Instead, ambition overwhelmed me, and I was unwilling to give up, fathoming I was demanding a blessing like Jacob wrestling at Peniel. Hardly. His patience was up.

My friend Angel disciplines her children when they speak to her disrespectfully. We hung out together just last night, and I watched her rebuke a particularly awful statement her older son aimed her way. Then, she explained to me, "They forget who they're talking to, who they are." That's exactly what happened to me. I forgot I'm the child (who's hardly a child anymore) and the Lord's the King of Kings. I spoke ridiculously to Him in the casual presumption that He'd overlook my robust "attitude" for having loved me in His own generosity as a friend.

Now, on top of cheating on love, I trampled respect and honor, much less the reverence due Him. He warned me: *Now you deserve hell.* Essentially, He seemed to be saying—people are suffering there for the same sins, and why should you be any different? You're forgetting reality—I'm in charge of your soul you don't control. You've forgotten who you're talking to how.

There's a verse in Matthew that says in the end, the Lord will basically say to many who will be surprised by His rejection, "Get thee away from me, evildoer. I never knew you." They will say, "But, Lord, we prophesied in Your name, we healed others in Your name, we ate and drank with You, we talked with You in the streets," and so on. Yet, they will go to hell. It was shortly after this warning that I was given that experience of terror in my sleep.

Since all this, the Lord's shown me what life apart from His Kingdom might be like. It's awful. I would have no idea what to do with myself. I've pursued His Kingdom for years. My entire support community consists of people of faith. I've spent all my spare time studying scripture or listening to and watching Christian media. I have been volunteering at a church clothing pantry each week for the last year and a half. The women there are like a family to me.

I can't imagine life without all these people suddenly, without focusing on God's will and way. I can't just go back to my former life! I would wish it were so easy. What a gift it is to be a part of His Kingdom! Indeed the woman living out of her car chasing conceits *with* the love of the King is *Rich Beyond Measure.* I was blind to the true reality and value, envying unbelievers, relatively unburdened as they may be by such testing and spiritual expectations.

So, here I am again, reaching from the pits to some hope of service. I know I need to humbly praise every day, exiled or not, for the hope of reconciling myself to His acceptance and love again. I need to live sacrificially and serve love despite my fall and compromise of my character. I must strive to build back what righteousness I can, hopefully earning His trust in my integrity over time. This much is certain: Despite the difficulty facing these consequences, I can't and wont give up.

Restoration

J UST WHEN I thought my relationship with God couldn't be darker, I got a call one bright Friday morning as I sat collecting pieces of self and life at Starbucks, again. My friend Irene was on the other end of the line informing me that she wanted to share something unusual. She said, "As soon as a I woke up this morning the Lord told me to pray for you." (Really?!) She went on, "So, I called up this prayer warrior friend of mine and we prayed for you." I told her, "You have no idea how badly I need that right now. I'm in it, Irene, deep."

For all the times I've prayed or someone else offered to pray for me and nothing came to pass, I've also experienced immediate supernatural answers to prayers that the Lord asks another to pray on my behalf. It's not happened very often, but I've seen powerful results when it does. Come to think of it, each time I've received some kind of immediate revelation of His presence to help me through the dark.

I unfolded the nature of my troubles to Irene. She listened intently to the story of my "fall" and lost calling and of the irreverence that cost me my security and standing in the Lord. To my surprise, she bluntly confronted me, "No, you haven't lost your salvation or your calling." I argued my case, my experiences. She insisted, "I know because I didn't know what I would say to you today. I asked the Spirit to guide me." As if that wasn't enough, in tandem with her words I experienced a confirming grace in my soul a moment later. As she shared a scripture, suddenly a light, bubbly joy-of-old distinctly arose in me. It carried with it a sense of prophecy, of a future season of loving immersion in the Bible. I was completely taken aback. Wow! What is going on here?

Unveiling my heavy story to my dear friend—well, I felt bad. I finally asked her how life was for her these days? Enough about me. Turns out, her mom was very sick. She asked me to pray for her healing. I agreed; although, inwardly, praying was the last thing I felt remotely qualified to do. We said our goodbyes. After we hung up, I was assured in the Spirit, *Go ahead and pray for her mom.* Ok...here goes! I said my prayer out loud, ending it in Jesus' good name. Weird and wrong as it all felt being the outcast I'd become, the "glory" fell down through the top of my head and spread throughout my body, ending with the goosebumps on my arms. I was informed my prayer was pleasing to the King. What on earth is going on?!

As I sat back down staring at my journal, my mind started racing, flooded with thoughts of hope. Suddenly a litany of questions came through—what if I might get to truly pray again someday? What if He might love me? What if I ever got the chance to marry Him again? What if I truly have a resurrected calling and hope of destiny? What if I may ever come to know the prayer that brought the tall man at church to tears that day? He was praying in the Spirit and suddenly began to declare the restoration of my original salvation. Surely, my mind was running down a road it shouldn't.

Later that night, as I sat doubting my worthiness of a miraculous restoration, His angels warned me, *You don't know what He's able to resurrect from the very pits of hell.* I argued: *But my sins are too grave. I gave my righteousness away. I'm not worthy or fit for the battle anymore.* Again, I got warned, *No, you don't get to judge that ultimately. You're as fit as God deems you, redeeming your righteousness daily. You don't get to just bow out of the battle. And yes, He's still able to make of you His instrument. You're gonna have to fight for it, but it's not over yet.*

I guess I thought it was over and done. I mean, I've heard countless people testifying God literally raises up the dead, whether it be flesh or the course of a failed or hell-bound life journey. He redeems things you couldn't imagine were remotely redeemable. I remember the testimony of one young man met by Jesus and sent back to life on earth after finding himself in the very pit of hell. He works miracles well beyond the amazing healing stories that get so much attention. None of this was lost on me, despite my faltering faith.

So, I considered all these turn of events. I'd been diligently searching counseling programs by the light of day, turning from the dark of the nights to seek a redemptive purpose for my life. I had begun falling in love with the thought of becoming a counselor. Now, here I was confronted with a whole host of other hopes and this renewed purpose in tow. Perhaps I'd be a pastor someday after all.

I began pleading with the Lord to create space in my future for this new angle I'd begun considering. I was honest with Him. I had never imagined being a pastor. It was never a purpose I had fathomed. And frankly, I found it intimidating. I have rarely seen female pastors in my church experience so I have little sense of myself in that position apart from want of communion with God in His will for me. However, becoming a counselor was my only competing consideration before entering education. I began to wonder, was this counseling thing a possible fruit born of the severity of pruning my calling? What exactly is God able to redeem and restore? Could I actually become both a counselor and a pastor?

As I interviewed counselors and visited local programs, I began sensing a dual course of study was overkill in the Lord's sight. Despite this, my wounded insecurity drove me on to scheme ways to work in both degrees. It would take longer, and I'm not getting any younger, nor am I getting richer. Practically speaking, I ought to choose one or the other.

The problem is, I don't trust this calling enough to put all my eggs in one basket. What if I invest years and dimes in this divinity degree and fall into spiritual trouble again that could keep me from working as a minister? It's not like I foresee intentionally sinning again, especially after my Eve lesson recently. Nevertheless, it was traumatizing to fall so hard from purpose to the pit.

Although many have been surprised by the severity of some of the consequences I've faced in my faith walk, there is a scripture in the letter to the Romans, in which Paul warns them about staying humble and grateful of the gravity of one's salvation. He states, *Note then the kindness and the severity of God: severity towards those who have fallen, but God's kindness towards you, provided you continue in his kindness; otherwise, you also will be cut off. Romans 11:22*

I've also been warned that a lot of the challenges I've faced have to do with the great degree of grace that was entrusted to me early on in my salvation. On this account, I failed high expectations and have suffered a measure of consequence in kind. In the gospel of Luke, Jesus warned, *From everyone to whom much has been given, much will be required; and from the one to whom much has been entrusted, even more will be demanded. Luke 12:48* At least a part of my difficulty has been according to the degree of power and the particular graces I received in getting saved.

One of these graces is the Lord's presence abiding with me. The other day, I asked Him why He still stays with me. I feel I've failed Him so badly sometimes that I'm honestly surprised He sticks around at all. He said, *For goodness sake.* That's such a relief to me. It is pure hope. Never as I do now, at this stage in my life's experiences, do I appreciate the great power of those three words: *For goodness sake.* Sometimes, everything just boils down to that one simple hope. May all the pain and heartache, all the struggle and strife, all the patient endurance, all the loss and all the climb—may it be for goodness sake. What truly matters, ultimately? Love.

Just this morning I was at breakfast with my family. It was a beautiful scene—the wall of windows filtering the morning sunlight across a big, open restaurant full of such diverse souls. In my imagination I saw Him walking gently amongst everyone, leaning into the crowd standing and waiting to be seated, people short and tall, to kiss their foreheads in love. He embodied an unassuming, but arresting stature. He was tall, robed in white, kind. Pure Majesty. I was struck with the longing to be one He loves also, to be like everyone around me. Suddenly, my heart gripped with grief I know to be His. I held back tears from my father's searching eyes, sitting next to me. I could clearly sense Jesus' love for me and sorrow at my reflection. I will try to remember this as I face every trauma and insecurity. Despite justice, He still loves me.

Written Not With Ink

Teach me your way, O LORD, that I may walk in your truth. Give me an undivided heart to revere your name.

Psalm 86:11

I JUST GOT FINISHED saying one thing. Now, I'm eating my own words. Always heed your angels, eh? Angels and God generally agree. They deliver His will to the world. He is the Lord of hosts, after all. Psalm 103:19-21 praises this reality justly stating, *The LORD has established his throne in the heavens, and his kingdom rules over all. Bless the LORD, O you his angels, you mighty ones who do his bidding, obedient to his spoken word. Bless the LORD, all his hosts, his ministers that do his will.* This never ceases to amaze me. Fathom, there are powerful angels watching over us in the will of a Heavenly Father. Amazing.

I realize, having never heard angels until after I put my faith in Jesus, how blessed I should be to receive any guidance or help at all, much less protection. Many times, the challenge of my life was knowing what God wants. Too often I've swirled about in the confusion of uncertainty. "Direction and clarity," my redundant prayer duo. Then, there are times He's clear as day, and it's a real challenge for me to obey. Despite heavenly warnings, I'm struggling to release the pursuit of counseling.

I also realized I had a massive blind spot in my decision making: the book! How did I neglect this? It's no small affair to aim to publish the intimate love and trial of one's relationship to God and life. Especially for the measure of failure I've sought to overcome. I quit my teaching job five years ago. I've only just begun pursuing schooling after years of questioning my salvation, looking for work, and searching for purpose. This isn't necessarily the stuff of a hero story for heaven's sake. It's just honest and well-meaning.

That said, my story matters to me especially in the sharing. Had I given remote consideration to this, perhaps I would have chosen to be that "woman of courage and integrity" the Lord called me to be instead of rationalizing a cheap date. Then, I'd still be true and faithful and pure towards the Man I always wanted to marry. I could have ended my book on a more victorious note, rather than a fall to the pit. But I wasn't thinking. I'm not writing a book I've forgotten I'm writing, I'm writing a life I didn't realize is a book.

Expressions are rolling through my mind. *The hairs of your head....* *The pages of your life....* are numbered? No no no. It's the *days* of your life are numbered, and the Lord knows each one. Nay, He's known and numbered your days before you even were. This is the word of comfort exchanged at times. This idea always bothered me. Life isn't so scripted. God surely loves free will and freedom too much.

I never thought my job as a nanny would make me think of His relation to man so much. When I pick up my kids each day: *What would you like to do today?* I tally each child's desires and calculate our logistical issues and concerns as best I can just to accommodate their heart and will. They lead, insofar as I'm able to defend it. I delight to delight them. Ice cream cones cost me a delicious three dollars at the Chick-fil-A drive-through just to see the kids so happy in the rear view mirror. They probably ought to be eating fruit, not ice cream; but hey, life feels sweeter when it's short. And I could swear I've felt this in the Lord when I splurge on them in my nanny-as-grandma treats.

When I first attempted to study religion at the state school, my advisor recommended I check out Bible colleges. Nevertheless, I insisted. This vision of an interdisciplinary degree possessed me. Five months into this program, I couldn't handle it anymore. I transferred to Christ for the Nations Institute. Why didn't the Lord warn me sooner Himself? Some would say, He did! Through your advisor. Ok, sure. But, if He chooses to say something to you explicitly... like, *Go to Starbucks.* A direct command. I say, That's nice Lord. I'd love a coffee, but I can do without it today. Thank You. I love You. *No, I said go to Starbucks.* Ok. Sure enough, I "run into" a friend I need to see for His purposes. Oh, oops.

So, if He guides me there, why not to CFNI? After many instances like this, I've decided He truly wanted to let my heart lead when it came to that decision about school. Then, I imagine how insanely dynamic He must be. And how He must effortlessly order everything according to His priorities in guiding and managing lives. Now that He's restored this calling to become a minister, my heart resists. War weary and wounded, I want solid ground. No risk worth taking rests on the solidity that I'm needing now. No calling He'd place upon me has any foundation apart from faith in Him. I know He's trustworthy, perfect in His will and way. Fallible as I may be, I can safely say I trust I will genuinely pursue His will and way. So, what's the problem?

Counseling, much as I was guided to it, is not the same path as becoming a pastor. It's not so incompatible necessarily, in the bigger picture; but, at this point I'm exerting my heart and will against heaven's wisdom, despite my warning to heed one's angels. He's willing to accommodate me, but I'm left to deal with my own fears of trying to become a pastor and my need for assurance in this new field of work and study. I'm hoping to adapt my future's vision for the sense of security this path offers me in the face of my fears.

On the one hand, I've got a sympathy for struggle I never imagined would grow quite so steep. Shortly after I dropped out of classes this last term, I decided I ought to check out the library and do some personal studying. From childhood, libraries seemed able to engulf me—endless potential to sate a hunger to learn. Not this day. Aisle after aisle lay dead, no pulse in any spine until…. Ah, the section about Suicide. Suddenly the place lit up. Sadly, I felt so relieved. Interest yet still lives in me! I checked several out and really read only one with any heart. It was a book of short testimonials by people who looked that Low in the eye and decided to trade out the period ending their story for a semi-colon, to continue on. "Project Semicolon," it was called.

As I read through these testimonies, I had to realize and accept, I'm another page in this book. I'm no different—I've had to choose life deliberately. I've had to choose my semi-colon again and again, deep in the despair of depression. I felt sympathy for the grief and suffering life can bring. Such trial and such tremendous resilience. Each soul speaks a story being lived against unseen forces and realities hard to express, impossible to capture, to truly do justice. Yet, each one of us is left to navigate, endure, and author our own story. At one point, my heart was overcome with His sorrow. In that moment, I felt Him convey to my soul a pleasure in my willingness to walk into the deep waters with people in need as a counselor. It may not be His exact will and desire. But, He was pleased in me nonetheless. I took heart.

Then, I think, should I really pursue the "wrong" career just to find security? Not if I'm writing the best life story. It's not how I ever chose to live before; but, now I'm seasoned in my willingness to take risks. I'm much older and life's lost some of the rush I felt in embracing hopes and dreams courageously. I want grit and ground now. Perhaps in time, with the solidity I crave sated, I will come to long for the leap-of-faith life again. Heaven knows I literally feel guilty because a handful of writers have spoken as much counsel into my life recently. I've been hitting up Barnes and Nobles to buy book after book. Now, I'm steeped in calls to write a life I'm proud of, one I truly enjoy, a life that makes the most of being alive.

The nobility of this cry confronts me just when I'm most pragmatically faithless. Now, I'm being asked by an angel, *What if you're depriving people of a pastor they need busy being a counselor?* What on earth?! That never would have occurred to me. Ever. Goodness… Well, I guess they're gonna have to wait for a grown up, able-to-stand-on-her-feet, spiritually strengthened, faith-healed woman to embrace becoming a pastor after gaining wisdom and experience as a counselor. It's gonna take longer, it's not heaven's idea of the best path to take, and I'll have to hold to a long range dream over time to get there, but ultimately I'll only be a stronger pastor for it. Says Reason. And that's the story I'm choosing to write!

How strange to craft stories of the future, of a purpose worth pursuing. There's no reason I can't write fresh purposes into my future by choice and commitment. That's the sense of autonomy and possibility that blows a fresh breeze across my cramped, narrow mind as I read these many new authors. For example, one highlights a story about a father that changes his daughter's story by giving her a different role to play—in a family that opens orphanages. Who conceives of life so poetically that it's more *real* than it is even extraordinary? I want that.

I also want God. There is nothing like discovering His desires, His heart, His will, His way, being with Him, along for His ride. Surrender. Turning over the pen to just be the page. It is a total gift to be so privileged. It's not a reality I've always had the chance to live by, but I've certainly tried to live in such a way as to be listening for Him, searching Him out in any given situation. For the time being, faith is going to have to set some stakes in the dirt. I hope He forgives me. If anyone can work crazy twists and turns together and fit all kinds of things into one life, it's God. I'm just gonna have to count on Him to pull this story off.

Ultimately, the best story is the one written by His Spirit as a work of love. I just want to be the subject. That's the ending I want well past any work, any book, any period I'd take back. Any ground I'd try to lay. Any faith I'd hope to heal. When all that's left is all that matters—Love. To write a life of love, a life born of an undivided heart.

Treasure Hidden

*The kingdom of heaven is like treasure hidden in a field,
which someone found and hid; then in his joy he goes and
sells all that he has and buys that field.*

Matthew 13:44

IN THIS PARABLE, Jesus compared the kingdom of heaven to a treasure. From the beginning of this book, I compared my heart to a plot of land with real estate that I had sold to my love for reading scripture. It cost me the love I owed my loved ones and God, ultimately. In this lesson I came to realize the heart is a limited landscape. While the ability to hold love may know no bound, the limits of life when it came to my time and attention shaped and reflected my affections, priorities, and how I spent the life and soul I've been granted.

The bank account of my heart's love is the steepest, richest, most significant wealth I've stewarded in this ordinary or extraordinary life. For starters, I only get so many days. Psalm 90:12 states, *Teach us to count our days that we may gain a wise heart.* The mercy dividing these days into chapters of life has sometimes left me wanting, wishing past the regret of lessons learned for a brighter future—as I do even now in the writing of this life story. Proverbs 17:3 says, *The crucible is for silver, and the furnace is for gold, but the LORD tests the heart.* Much of this story of faith details the trials I've endured in the testing of my heart. The heart is the true mind: sensing, perceiving, valuing, cherishing, rejecting, exercising all manners of intellect unavailable to any other aspect of one's being.

Proverbs 4:23 states, *Keep your heart with all vigilance, for from it flow the springs of life.* The question concluding this book and reflection on faith is this: *How do you choose to spend your heart in all the limits that shape life?* What does my love speak of life and how do I spend my love? I know that God's love spoke eternal life over me, a sinner, and He spent all His love on man's salvation. He purchased such grace in the ultimate sacrifice. Now, how will I purchase Him, my treasure? How do I spend all I have buying my field?

For many, marriage is the ultimate expression of love in life. This covenant is singular and defined by devotion and commitment, a vow and promise no force can separate. God agrees. Throughout scripture He refers to Himself in relation to man as "your Maker" and "Husband." For example, in Isaiah 54:5 He states: *For your Maker is your husband, the LORD of hosts is his name; the Holy One of Israel is your Redeemer, the God of the whole earth he is called.* Again, Jesus likened the gift of salvation to a marriage in Matthew 22:2 stating: *The kingdom of heaven may be compared to a king who gave a wedding banquet for his son.*

That king is the Father. This was God whom I knew as my friend as a child. There was a period of time in my early childhood when my mother had a habit of assigning two-hour naps each day after lunch to me and my sister. During this daily window of unreal exercise in childhood patience, I naturally had way too much energy to sleep, but had no choice but to pass two silent hours alone. I would play quietly with my dolls and recall talking with my friend, God, throughout this play time. With no education, I knew He was a "father" I couldn't see but was every bit real. In fact, I used to wonder why He never seemed to tire of me.

At some point I lost this awareness of Him and entered into the lengthiest phase of my life in a godless sense of privacy and independence. It wasn't until I was confronted by my need for God at various turns, faced as I was by justice and my need for salvation in all my straying, that I ended up giving thought to God. In Luke 15:3-5, He says: *"Which one of you having a hundred sheep and losing one of them, does not leave the ninety-nine in the wilderness and go after the one that is lost until he finds it? When he's found it, he lays it on his shoulders and rejoices."* All my life, despite my straying, the Lord was faithful to go after me time and again until I was found.

In the earlier part of my story, I shared about the beginning of my faith walk, before I was confronted with trial and consequence. I had entered into this marriage to my Savior in the commitment I made at my baptism. Specifically, I stated that day to those witnessing at church that I would commit each day of my life to serving Him in gratitude for His love and redemption. As His brides-to-be, He warned believers about their journey in the parable of the ten bridesmaids in the book of Matthew: *Then the kingdom of heaven will be like this. Ten bridesmaids took their lamps and went to meet the bridegroom. Five of them were foolish, and five were wise... Matthew 25:1-2*

As the story goes, the foolish didn't invest in flasks of oil to see the bridegroom's arrival should he arrive in the night, but the wise did. As the bridegroom was delayed, the foolish didn't have sufficient oil to keep their lamps lit, so they went back to purchase more from town and missed His arrival in the night. The wise women entered the wedding banquet ready, and the foolish were turned away on their return because the Lord claims He never knew them.

That may seem harsh, but it's a testament of faithlessness ultimately. To know God is to love Him truly in the manner that honors His true love. While I believe I have loved God genuinely, my story has been one of lessons learned. I was a well-meaning, yet foolish bridesmaid. My salvation came into question as I divided my heart's affections after receiving the gift of grace I first knew.

Ingratitude took hold of my soul as I slowly suffered consequences over time and lost grace after grace. I slid further into sin, looking back constantly at what I once knew in sorrow and bitterness of loss. Despite the seeming humanity in this reaction, my sins dealing with my circumstance brought justice alongside a lot of mercy. So, mine is a story of salvation eight years ago, shipwrecked faith in the last few years, and now, a hope for restoration by the grace and mercy of my God.

Nonetheless, this oil the bridesmaids keep to light their wait for the groom is more than just a symbol in a parable. It's referencing the actual flame of love in the heart "chakra"—the "Christ-light" as some call it. So, the oil—the anointing of the Spirit—lights the lamp of His presence in one's heart. I can testify of this quite literally—I've felt my heart both burn with heat and suffer the pain of an ice-cold absence of His heat as well. I know by His revelation that the cold I felt was meant to demonstrate to me His displeasure by depriving me of His warmth and presence, by withdrawing His "oil." It was a temporary experience but quite eye-opening, nonetheless.

Proverbs 13:9 says, *The light of the righteous rejoices, but the lamp of the wicked goes out.* This is a literal reality I always took for granted prior to knowing a direct relationship to Christ in the spirit. I've experienced the literal and true hardening of my heart over time. The pain and empathy I once felt became desensitized. My testimony is not ideal, but unfortunate, and a warning, ultimately. It is supremely important to guard one's lamp and to keep that flask of oil. To be a bridesmaid eagerly awaiting her King is but the beginning of the honor due such a wedding as this.

Ode to a Capable Wife

PROVERBS CHAPTER 31 has a lengthy ending devoted to the praises of a perfect wife called "Ode to a Capable Wife." If a devoted bridesmaid waits prepared for the bridegroom's arrival, what sort of bride-to-be honors the Lord? The Capable Wife paints a vivid picture for us of devotion and love. The Ode starts, *10 A capable wife who can find? She is far more precious than jewels. 11 The heart of her husband trusts in her, and he will have no lack of gain. 12 She does him good, and not harm, all the days of her life.* The believer's call is devotion to serving the Lord in trustworthy love. One's call is to bring the Lord gain and do Him good all our days, to be loyal.

I think back to the experience I had drinking for the first time after I'd put away alcohol for the first eight months of my commitment. I was in a rich communion with His spirit then. I distinctly felt I was disloyal, unfaithful as my sobriety slipped away. It was a clear infidelity to give away any part of my sober communion with His spirit. It makes me realize why God called consecrated servants like John the Baptist and Samson to abstain from alcohol. There is simply no communion between His spirit and strong drink. In my double-minded naïveté, I didn't value His presence as He deserved.

Also, I bent to a sense of peer pressure around old friends. Proverbs 25:26 states, *Like a muddied spring or a polluted fountain are the righteous who give way before the wicked.* My "righteousness" was a gift to me from the Lord. I was no more righteous or worthy of this title than the "wicked" before whom I gave way. Nevertheless, I forsook an opportunity to stand my ground in love for God and my friends. I could have reflected the way of life and well being, of satisfaction in God. Instead, I bent towards them, not God, to try to bridge the gap of misunderstanding between us. I was unfaithful to the Lord. Though I have since changed, how I wish I had lived out fidelity to the Spirit I once knew. He is precious beyond compare. I couldn't have fathomed Him justly then. I was ignorant and took Him for granted. Now I long for what I once knew, hoping my lessons might save another my heartache and failure.

Despite the learning curve I've experienced in that ignorance, the call to fidelity is for "all the days of her life." Faithful is constant, just as the Lord's love is deemed steadfast in so many psalms, enduring forever. I have discernment now. Those I see who guarded the gift they received in the beginning shine as bright as ever to this day. They are not awaiting a hope of restoration. I can see clearly they simply rested in God's initial grace. How worthy such a wisdom is in the fruit she bears! Thus, faithful is the capable wife.

Furthermore, she brings the Lord "gain" in all these days. How do you increase God's gain day by day? What can I give God daily? My heart, mind, and soul. But, what does it mean? In my heart, I discovered while teaching to set aside an hour each morning to love and worship Him through music. This practice strengthened my walk through the day tremendously. I devoted the next hour to studying scripture, especially the epistles. This fixed my mind on the call to purity of character these texts emphasize.

Finally, I tried to pull this focus of heart and mind into my effort to teach and reach each child as fully as I could through the day. I think that effort comes from the soul. At the minimum I was able to give God that much faithful devotion each day. This season was the healthiest of my entire faith walk because of this devotion and faithfulness, despite its torments, and even despite what infidelities I may have committed in my naïveté and ignorance. In the subsequent season of my salvation's insecurity, a lot of this devotion fell away as I was confronted by insecurity, demonization, and judgment.

I honestly spent so much time loving and adoring a God I was grateful to with all my heart. When that love gets wounded, it's hard to go on in it, harder to worship or listen to the same songs and express my heart like I once knew. Keeping that love alive and nurtured is the most important devotion, but it's sensitive and subject to wounding. I have, for what it's worth, stayed committed to study of the Word and a daily effort to live as righteously as I can.

What does that righteousness look like? Let's continue studying the capable wife. The next verses state: *13 She seeks wool and flax, and works with willing hands. 14 She is like the ships of the merchant, she brings her food from far away. 15 She rises while it is still night and provides food for her household and tasks for her servant girls.* Thus, she works hard without complaint and goes to great length to provide for her household.

It's interesting to me that providing was not simply the province of a husband, but also the duty of the wife. She is expected to participate in the work it takes to provide by seeking food and materials from afar—out in the city. She is hardly confined to the home. In fact, she has servant girls and is a fair and responsible supervisor of her home's staff.

If that's not sufficient incentive to be a thorough, diligent, and hard worker, there's a proverb that likens a slack worker to a thief. I'm working in the farm kitchen a few days a week. Each time I see a corner with that broom in my hand and I consider the ambiguous and possibly useless effort to reach into it for nothing, I think of these types of verses and try to press into it. I debate it mentally—*but there is no dirt there!*

Yet, diligence speaks to the effort above and beyond. Minute as this example may be, I've literally felt the Lord's pleasure in some simple morning when I manage to make several of these decisions righteously. Despite my struggles, a string of such choices produced in me the distinct awareness that He was pleased with me. I learned that each small choice truly matters, and much more so than I'd imagine or fathom crediting.

Oh, how good it feels to be in His pleasure! So, we continue to study the traits of a good wife. The next verses state: *16 She considers a field and buys it; with the fruit of her hands she plants a vineyard. 17 She girds herself with strength, and makes her arms strong. 18 She perceives that her merchandise is profitable. Her lamp does not go out at night.* These verses are really interesting to me in that she clearly has and uses strong business sense. She deals financially of her own wisdom and strength, and she knows her worth is great. She doesn't sell short in weak insecurity.

So much of one's security in this faith walk comes by knowing your worth in Christ and standing in that worth in your integrity of character. If He suffered the cross for your sake—your life, future, health, prosperity, freedom, and destiny—then, you sure are worth an awful lot.

To lay down that worth for something unworthy is a waste of all the goodness purchased sacrificially for the sake of your well being. When I chose to drink again, I traded that goodness for a superficial, temporary release and escape from discomfort and pain. I traded what was worth much for what was actually costly in the long run. This woman, this capable wife, knows better. She wouldn't allow such an exchange to bring down her profit—she knows her merchandise is truly expensive.

Furthermore, her lamp does not go out at night. Not only does she work long hours, for all that worth is earned legitimately, but also, just like the wise bridesmaid, she doesn't run out of oil waiting for her groom. The irony! I was unwittingly tempted by the potential for a marriage to come of meeting the young man from earlier in my story. It just so happened we met in the same term when I could-have, should-have been attending the district grant I'd won.

I ended up distracted by this new, exciting relationship I never expected—a companionship that brought much comfort and encouragement in the face of trial and torment. Yet, I didn't earn the reward, ultimately, as my time and attention ended up divided. There simply was not enough genuine work or effort invested in the class. I didn't appreciate the temptation I was faced with and the fact that blessings come with testing. I was young in the faith and lacked wisdom. Fortunately, my lessons learned could be another's opportunity to rise and shine.

The next verses show her fashion sense. She knows how to dress, and she creates the clothing that she and her family wear. *19 She puts her hands to the distaff, and her hands hold the spindle. 20 She opens her hand to the poor, and reaches out her hands to the needy. 21 She is not afraid for her household when it snows, for all her household are clothed in crimson. 22 She makes herself coverings; her clothing is fine linen and purple... 25 Strength and dignity are her clothing, and she laughs at the time to come.* Her fate is in her hands and her hands are in control—confident and deliberate. She is so abundantly supplied in her prosperity that her generosity gives in charity. She is wealthy, compassionate, and wise inside and out.

Twice I had hoped to help a sister in need, and twice I learned generosity takes wisdom. In one instance, I tried to help a woman from my Bible study save money. She was staying in a month-to-month hotel which was quite expensive. I was still teaching then and had a spare bedroom. I invited her to stay a couple of weeks to save money. After a week I realized we couldn't get along *at all*. I ended up fulfilling my promise by paying for her to stay at a motel. I'm ashamed of this, yet I learned you shouldn't make a promise to someone you don't know well enough.

In the second instance, I got along really well with a woman I met at a soup kitchen. She was living out of her van. She was a reverend who knew the Word extremely well. I was amazed and hungry for insight. After a week she confided in me that she was being persecuted. This man had already threatened her—showing her how he was very able to locate her by her car. Considering her car stood out in our parking lot, this freaked me out. I decided she was safer to stay at the local Salvation Army where she could blend in the group and be with some authorities. Yet, I broke my vow again.

Proverbs 22:26 states, *Do not be one of those who gives pledges, who become surety for debts.* So, I learned this a second time. After spending a good deal on clothing and hopes to promote her ability to find work, I asked her to leave. My heart rejected the responsibility of keeping her. I felt I couldn't afford this as I was trying to focus on succeeding in my efforts at UNT. I hated breaking my promise which I've learned was still the greater sin than making it. I vowed not to make vows in the future, and I regretted asking her to leave.

Proverbs 19:17 says, *Whoever is kind to the poor lends to the LORD, and will be repaid in full.* Despite my errors in lending, I was helped out on one occasion when I needed a place to crash on short notice and a fellow sister invited me into her home. I ended up in a beautiful short-term friendship staying with her for a time. So, I was indeed repaid in full for my giving. Nevertheless, I learned many lessons about the nature of giving and generosity. The Lord was not pleased I failed to honor His servants who I asked to leave early. I also shouldn't have spent the money I did in the way I did. A well meaning wife I may have been, yet lacking in the wisdom of financial stewardship the capable wife exercises. She is shrewd when it comes to managing her family's possessions and finances and wise in giving to the poor.

At last, even when it's cold and her family may be facing hardship, they're dressed in crimson, covered in the blood of Christ. They have their refuge in the spiritual covering of the Lord's favor, clothed in "fine linen and purple," the royal garb of the bride of a King. They have the true wealth, the spiritual safety and provision that sustains you in times of trial. This woman is not only shrewd in managing her wealth materially, but also spiritually. In this she provides for her family as well.

She "laughs at the time come," secure in her sense of the future because she is behind the shield of the Lord. Psalm 18:30 states, ...*the promise of the Lord proves true; he is a shield for all who take refuge in him.* And Psalm 5:12 states, *For you bless the righteous, O LORD; you cover them with favor as with a shield.*

With All Wisdom and Insight

FINALLY, THIS WIFE is wise, kind, and humble. *26 She opens her mouth with wisdom, and the teaching of kindness is on her tongue... 30 Charm is deceitful, and beauty is vain, but a woman who fears the LORD is to be praised. 31 Give her a share in the works of her hands, and let her works praise her in the city gates.*

Wisdom is paramount in the scriptures and key to living the path and way of life. Proverbs 3:15 states, *She is more precious than jewels, and nothing you desire can compare with her.* She is said to watch over you and keep you, to speak to you in the morning when you wake. Wisdom is compared to a woman who stood by the Lord's side as His first work and His companion as He created the heavens and the earth. Proverbs 3:19-20 states, *The LORD by wisdom founded the earth; by understanding he established the heavens; by his knowledge the deeps broke open, and the clouds drop down the dew.*

And in her own words, she states in Proverbs 8: *22 The LORD created me at the beginning of his work, the first of his acts of long ago. 23 Ages ago I was set up, at the first, before the beginning of the earth... 25 Before the mountains had been shaped... 27 When he established the heavens... 28 when he made firm the skies above... 29 when he assigned to the sea its limit, so the waters might not transgress his command... 30 then I was beside him, like a master worker; and I was daily his delight, rejoicing before him always, rejoicing in his inhabited world and delighting in the human race.*

Wisdom is called a fountain of life. Of wisdom, Proverbs 4:8-9 states,

Prize her highly, and she will exalt you; she will honor you if you embrace her. She will place on your head a fair garland; she will bestow on you a beautiful crown. In other words, she will grant you beauty of thought and mind. She will prepare you in royal garb for marriage to a King. She will give you the mind of Christ.

For all my struggles trying to please God in the face of my errors and trials, I have been blessed at times for having developed a measure of insight. He has pointed out particular proverbs to me to indicate— *that's you in My sight.* Proverbs 15:23 states, *To make an apt answer is a joy to anyone, and a word in season, how good it is!* Furthermore, Proverbs 16:24 states, *Pleasant words are like a honeycomb, sweetness to the soul and health to the body.* Oddly, I was surprised when He showed me that encouraging words please Him and "bring down the glory." That phenomena is what happens when that rush of cool, refreshing air falls on you from above soaking into your body, giving goosebumps and feeling generally great. That's His spirit and pleasure, and it's healing to the flesh. What a strange and neat insight—how accurate the Bible can be!

My favorite is Proverbs 22:11 which states, *Those who love a pure heart and are gracious in speech will have the king as a friend.* What a blessing is that! Despite my struggles, I've known this blessing at times. He's been my friend and shared His joy and humor and laughter with me. It is sweet and like nothing else. Despite my trials, I count myself immensely blessed to have ever known this joy. Finally, Proverbs 16:13 states, *Righteous lips are the delight of a king, and he loves those who speak what is right.* Again, imagine delighting the King with your words—how amazing is that?! Wow.

Oh, to be loved by God and to bring Him delight! Proverbs 12:4 states, *A good wife is the crown of her husband...* Isaiah describes this and likens the bride-to-be to a royal marriage in chapter 62, verses 3 and 5: *You shall be a crown of beauty in the hand of the LORD, a royal diadem in the hand of your God... For as a young man marries a young woman, so shall your builder marry you, and as the bridegroom rejoices over the bride, so shall your God rejoice over you.*

So is the reward of the believer and bride-to-be, faithful and true to her King. She will be the delight of her Maker and will also herself rejoice in her God. Isaiah 61:10-11 states: *I will greatly rejoice in the LORD, my whole being shall exult in my God; for he has clothed me with the robe of righteousness, as a bridegroom decks himself with a garland, and as a bride adorns herself with her jewels. For as the earth brings forth its shoots, and as a garden causes what is sown in it to spring up, so the Lord GOD will cause righteousness and praise to spring up before all the nations.*

So God will raise up His church before the eyes of the world to see her in all her beauty, the work of the Holy Spirit in the heart and mind and soul of the believer to reflect His light and righteousness for all to see. *For the creation waits with eager longing for the revealing of the children of God... in hope that the creation itself will be set free from its bondage to decay and will obtain the freedom of the the glory of the children of God. Romans 8:19-21*

What greater treasure than this?

St. Paul spoke of his brethren in his letter to the Corinthian church: *You yourselves are our letter, written on our hearts to be known and read by all; and you show that you are a letter of Christ, prepared by us, written not with ink but with the Spirit of the living God, not on tablets of stone but on tablets of human hearts... And all of us, with unveiled faces, seeing the glory of the Lord as though reflected in a mirror, are being transformed into the same image from one degree of glory to another... 2 Corinthians 3:2-18*

The church and the believer reflect the Word of God for the world to know God the Father and the Son and the Spirit whom would remain unknown but for the sharing of the faith. What precious grace to know our Maker through one another. What precious grace to understand Him by the work of His Spirit poured out on man. What precious grace was purchased at such great price as to esteem His treasure, mankind, to the utmost.

St. Paul exhorted in the letter to the Ephesians, *In him we have redemption through his blood, the forgiveness of our trespasses, according to the riches of his grace that he lavished on us. With all wisdom and insight he has made known to us the mystery of his will, according to his good pleasure set forth in Christ, as a plan for the fullness of time, to gather up all things in him, things in heaven and things on earth. Ephesians 1:7-10*

At the end of the road, my story of a faith walk begun in tremendous blessing and beset with trials and lessons learned, comes to a close standing at the edge of that field. I had hoped to buy this field with the treasure of salvation I buried in it. I ask you, reader, consider the gift of salvation God has offered us in Christ. Proverbs 20:20 states, *Who can say, "I have made my heart clean; I am pure from my sin"?* Yet, by His precious blood shed for us, we can be made clean and come into fellowship with our Maker and brethren. By faith and the gift of His Spirit we can make Him known to others and shine His light.

Imagine the great gift this is, that the salvation of one's own soul is also one's great glory before the ultimate majesty of our Maker. Psalm 8 states: *3 When I look at your heavens, the work of your fingers, the moon and the stars that you have established; 4 what are human beings that you are mindful of them, mortals that you care for them? 5 Yet you have made them a little lower than God, and crowned them with glory and honor.*

So, with gratitude for your commitment to reading my story through, I urge you: Take this treasure, this ultimate gift of God, and cherish it with all you have as a bride faithful to her King. As Paul said in 2 Timothy 1: 14, *Guard the good treasure entrusted to you.* Sell all you have for the soil and ground that keeps it precious, hidden, forever buried in your heart.

Finally, Psalm 24: 9-10 exhorts, *Lift up your heads, O gates! And be lifted up, O ancient doors! That the King of glory may come in. Who is the King of glory? The LORD of hosts, he is the King of glory.* Look to the heavens with open eyes, gazing through the light of an open heart and mind. Realize there is a King with a host of angels ruling and reigning as a Savior Judge over all that you've known and seen. He's loved you to the greatest extent, covering His creation completely. Cherish this great gift of salvation. Prize it always, for it has ultimately prized you.

Bless the LORD, O my soul,
And all that is within me,
Bless his holy name.
Bless the LORD, O my soul,
And do not forget all his benefits—
Who forgives all your iniquity,
Who heals all your diseases,
Who redeems your life from the Pit,
Who crowns you with
Steadfast love and mercy,
Who satisfies you with good
As long as you live...
Psalm 103:1-5

Acknowledgments

First, I want to thank you, reader, for hearing my story and offering your time and consideration. I hope I made it worth your while, and I'm grateful for your patience, understanding, and care towards so much that took courage to express and share openly.

I also want to thank all the beautiful souls that contributed their hearts and minds not only to the diligent effort to polish the text in this book and to strengthen its content; but also, these people stood by my side and spoke love and grace into my life. My writers group, the "Greenliners," spoke hope over me and came alongside me in this faith journey.

I also want to thank my friends Andrea and Mark. You have been such a support and encouragement. You believe in me no matter what. What a gift your faith in me has been. I am grateful for you. Irene, thank you for holding me up. Your faith inspires me, and you were my landing spot just when I needed it most. I am grateful for you.

I want to thank the beautiful staff of Marcus High School for blessing my life's journey beyond measure. Thank you Kathy and Julie for mentoring me and loving me truly.

Finally, I am grateful for the devoted love and support of my dear family. I love you Mom, Dad, and Sister. You are God's first and great gift to my life. I pray you are kept always in His love and blessing. Thank you.

Thank You, Lord, for being with me and helping me. I love You.

Printed in the United States
By Bookmasters